SKIING

INTO   THE

BRIGHT
OPEN

Also Published by the University of Minnesota Press

No Horizon Is So Far: Two Women and
Their Historic Journey across Antarctica

Liv Arnesen and Ann Bancroft, with Cheryl Dahle

SKIING
INTO THE
BRIGHT
OPEN

MY SOLO JOURNEY
TO THE SOUTH POLE

LIV ARNESEN

FOREWORD BY ANN BANCROFT
TRANSLATED BY ROLAND HUNTFORD

UNIVERSITY OF MINNESOTA PRESS
MINNEAPOLIS
LONDON

Published by the University of Minnesota Press
111 Third Avenue South, Suite 290
Minneapolis, MN 55401-2520
http://www.upress.umn.edu

ISBN 978-1-5179-1149-2 (pb)
Library of Congress record available at https://lccn.loc.gov/2020053656.

Printed in the United States of America on acid-free paper

The University of Minnesota is an equal-opportunity educator and employer.

26 25 24 23 22 21   10 9 8 7 6 5 4 3 2 1

The one who has felt the eternal receding circle of the horizon has understood the essence of freedom, never to be satisfied but always to move the boundaries further out somewhere.

—Nordahl Grieg

CONTENTS

FOREWORD

Ann Bancroft

At long last, the story of Liv Arnesen's groundbreaking expedition to the South Pole has been published in English to share with an entirely new audience. First published in Norway in 1995, this account of a remarkable history-making solo adventure is told with understated grace by a no less remarkable woman.

Liv recounts her journey from dream to reality through her journal entries. Inspired by the polar history she loves, Liv weaves the tapestry of her endeavor with those who went before—combining her own life experiences both on and off the

Liv Arnesen and Ann Bancroft. Photograph by Isabel M. Subtil.

ice. Through these stories, we come to see just how Liv's mind and spirit work.

I first met Liv in 1998 when she took me up on an invitation to come to Minnesota and talk about a project I was launching to cross Antarctica. We knew of each other despite the ocean between us. In 1992–93, I had led a team of American women to the South Pole. And as this book details, Liv would follow solo and unsupported the following season. At the time, only a few women around the globe were pushing into the male domain of the polar regions, so we found it easy to learn about each other.

My goal in the early 1990s was to cross the continent of Antarctica, inspired as a girl by the book *Endurance* about Ernest Shackleton's ill-fated attempt to do the same in 1914–15. Like Liv, I experienced an insurmountable wall to getting the project funded. Convincing possible sponsors with societal norms in the boardrooms to follow our dreams was considerably harder than life on the ice. Climbing over the attitudinal barriers about what women can and cannot do was far more arduous than the sastrugi and headwinds that Antarctica would dish out.

Grassroots support from people who believed in four women would get us funded as far as the South Pole in 1992–93, but our hopes of changing corporate America's mind once we had made our midway point at the Pole and proved our mettle did not, ultimately, loosen the needed sponsorship dollars for the second half of our journey across the continent.

Before leaving the South Pole for home, through tears of disappointment, I would scratch new plans in the back of my journal for returning for the traverse. My plan called for trimming the team to just two people to move fast and efficiently. Although our team returned home to a fanfare of delight and celebration as the first women to ski to the South Pole, I had colliding feelings of success and failure that only I seemed to possess. People were thrilled by our achievement, and the goal of the traverse was all but forgotten. I would have to trust that one day my time would come again to actualize the full dream.

That time did finally arrive. Seven years later, seduced by the wide-open expanses, I started to lay the framework—not just on the ice but in the marketing departments that could help support efforts both on the journey and in classrooms around the world. I would no longer wait for those who dared not step into the future.

With no aspirations for a solo crossing, I began to think of a teammate. I immediately thought of Liv, remembering how beautifully she had executed her South Pole expedition. I have often joked that if one is seeking success in the polar regions, partner with a Norwegian—and in this case it's no joke, and Liv is so much more. Having joined the ranks of Nansen and Amundsen as a skilled, strong skier who executed an almost flawless expedition and having traveled alone for fifty days, she proved she could be self-sufficient and, just as important, enjoy herself while doing it. These were qualities I felt necessary for a team of just two.

Meeting her for the first time, however, I was totally intimidated, and rather than exuding confidence when I met her at the airport I became totally shy. Once we began to walk and talk, fortunately, my shyness faded and was replaced by excitement of the possibilities we could achieve together.

We discovered on our walks that we were both drawn to the outdoors and sport at an early age and that we both had parents who nurtured their unusual daughters. We discovered that the same books of early polar expeditions had fed our imaginations of beautiful, distant, and vast icescapes. We'd both become educators, and as women of polar firsts, we each felt a stir to use the platform we felt so privileged to stand on in a larger, more sustainable way.

This awakening to pushing boundaries beyond the physical

and geographical had started for me after standing at the North Pole in 1986, the first known woman to do so. I felt a strong pull at the time to use the flurry of attention from my accomplishment to do something within my passion but bigger than myself and my personal ambitions. When I launched our all-women's trip to Antarctica in 1992, I followed through on this promise by developing curriculum to help share the journey and inspire young people to their own dreams and potential. While listening to Liv talk about her feelings coming home from her solo journey, and how she felt similar desires to broaden the work beyond herself, I knew she was beyond perfect as a teammate for the biggest challenge of my career. These similarities began to forge our friendship with a bedrock foundation—of certainly our passions but also now of a larger purpose.

Liv's account of her time on the ice gives the reader a solid sense of the woman I have been fortunate to travel with on many expeditions for more than two decades. Her towering inner strength, her courage and calm in the face of adversity, and her endless curiosity about what's over the horizon all make for an amazing expedition. She overcomes not only the obstacles of the continent but also those of cultural, sexist, and economic prejudices in pursuing her dreams, motivated by a passion for life and a desire to share it to make the world a better place.

Liv writes with a direct style and an attention to detail. Her ability to be present in the landscape and the space around her created a sense of peace in the silent expanse for fifty days. This can belie the hazards and the margin of error of being alone, but it speaks volumes to her comfort in wild spaces and with herself. Liv's story, like her place in history, will stand the test of time.

Perhaps the biggest discovery for me in rereading Liv's account is that while growing up I held dreams seemingly no one else shared—and now I have learned over the thin line of the horizon that there was another. My soul sister.

PROLOGUE

Christmas Eve. The Amundsen-Scott Base has been visible for five hours. The dome grows bigger, and more and more buildings appear. I cross the landing strip, and for the first time on the whole tour, I feel my skis gliding and make my first double heave on the poles.

It's four o'clock in the afternoon, Chilean time, which I've been following throughout my expedition. At home in Norway it's eight o'clock in the evening, and people are perhaps just finishing Christmas dinner. The Amundsen-Scott Base follows New Zealand time, so here it's actually early in the morning on Christmas Day.

At the ceremonial South Pole

The gleaming blue dome of the base, all the lines of tents, and the many cargo depots strewn around form a striking contrast to the image I have on my retina of Amundsen and his men standing at attention before their tent and the flag.

I see the dome on my right. On my left, I notice the well-known sign at the geographical South Pole. I haven't a single thought in my head, but ten meters from the geographical point the emotions rise. The tears stream during the last few meters to the Pole, and when I arrive I lean over my ski poles and cry my heart out.

I have nursed this dream for so long that I am quite prepared for my arrival at the South Pole to be an anticlimax. My thoughts are with those at home—I'm profoundly happy for their sake. Soon they will be able to relax and enjoy Christmas. The Americans at the base will send a message to Patriot Hills Base Camp, and the news of my arrival will quickly be relayed to Norway. At last I can be certain that Einar, and everyone else at home, will know that all is well. I've sent my reports, as agreed, every single day for fifty days, but I have no idea whether they got through.

It's been a wonderful experience to be a lonely nomad in Antarctica. The days passed incredibly quickly, though I do remember the overwhelming fatigue and emptiness of the first few days.

I sense another kind of emptiness now, as if something has been lost. Mentally, I feel as if I still have enormous reserves. I feel privileged to have gone through this experience—above all, to have realized a dream.

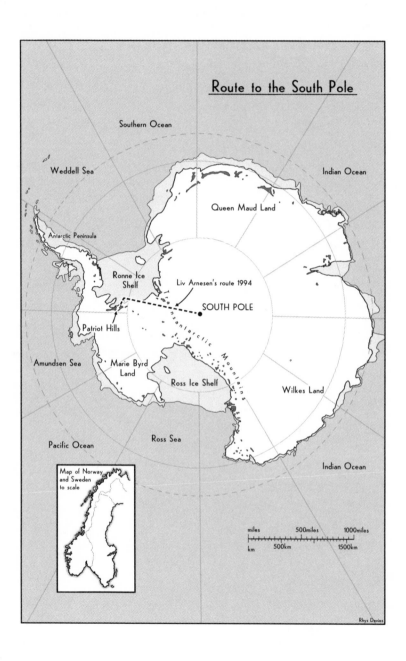

Route to the South Pole

Southern Ocean

Weddell Sea

Indian Ocean

Queen Maud Land

Antarctic Peninsula

Ronne Ice
Shelf

Liv Arnesen's route 1994

SOUTH POLE

Patriot Hills

Amundsen Sea

Marie Byrd
Land

Ross Ice Shelf

Wilkes Land

Pacific Ocean

Ross Sea

Indian Ocean

Map of Norway
and Sweden
to scale

miles   500miles   1000miles

km   500km   1500km

Rhys Davies

FRUIT IS BEST
ENJOYED WHEN RIPE

As I look back now on my expedition to the South Pole in 1994, it seems rather strange that it took so long before I dared set out on my long journeys. By the time I was twenty years old, I had enjoyed extensive, varied experiences in the outdoors—but it wasn't until I was thirty-seven that I made my first attempt to cross Greenland.

Why had I waited so long?

Long before my own trip to Greenland, I had read about Carl Emil Petersen, the Norwegian who accomplished the first solo crossing of Greenland on skis. Why hadn't I simply followed his example? I had dreamed of the South Pole since I was quite young, so why hadn't I set off earlier? In retrospect, there were many reasons—one of the most important being that I wasted many years discussing and planning with men.

The first modern South Pole expeditions I read about were the expedition of Roger Meare, Robert Swan, and Gareth Wood in 1985, recounted in *In the Footsteps of Scott*; Monica Kristensen's abortive attempt in 1989; and the journey by Will Steger and his international party in 1990, detailed in *Crossing Antarctica*. All these expeditions had insanely high budgets, which perhaps convinced me that it was better to let my dream remain a dream. The turning point came when another Norwegian, Erling Kagge, made the first solo journey to the South Pole, which he did with apparent ease, and kept to a reasonable budget in the bargain. I knew I was just as good a skier as Erling was and at least as experienced on glaciers.

Did I really want to go to the South Pole, or did I prefer to continue dreaming? It wasn't an academic question. I should explain something about our national psyche: many Norwegians have a tendency to live in the twilight world between imagination and reality and sometimes to confuse the two. In fact, one of Ibsen's great dramas, *Peer Gynt,* is based on this theme.

I often wonder what finally enabled me to escape from that twilight world and turn my dream into a concrete plan. It was a plan that required relentless training, extensive practical preparation, and a great deal of drudgery—all of which wasn't easy to fit in with a full-time job and my other responsibilities.

In the oft-quoted words of Ecclesiastes, "To every thing there is a season, and a time to every purpose under the heaven." Perhaps the answer is simply that, earlier, the time just wasn't right. The older you grow, the better you know yourself. Eventually, or at least hopefully, you discover your own ability and your own talents. Everyone is capable of something: some are skilled with their hands; others with their brains; still others with their legs. It's inspiring to seize an opportunity if you believe in it. You might not succeed, but in any case you will have tried.

It's been said that today's mental ability is tomorrow's agility. Everyone derives pleasure and use from some form of mental training; it's helped me enormously in a variety of circumstances. There are various methods, and since we're all different, each of us has to discover what suits us best.

As a result of injury, I had back trouble when I was young. It recurred when I started my studies at the Norwegian School of Sport Sciences, but by means of autogenic training I diverted attention from the back pain to something else. I repeated the syllabus by heart, or I immersed myself in a daydream. My attention didn't always circle around the South Pole, but I was nearly always out on some faraway journey or other.

The worst betrayal is the one committed against yourself by ignoring your abilities. It's just as important to respect yourself as it is to respect others. If you constantly feel that you're compromising with yourself, it's difficult to mean anything to others. I hope that my ski tour to the South Pole may prove to others, especially young women, that most things are possible, even when they venture into strange arenas. To fulfill a dream, it must be converted into a goal, so that one may start planning. Hard work then follows. Most ambitions can be realized, as long as your motives are strong enough—and genuine.

SKI TOURING BETWEEN THE COVERS OF A BOOK

Ever since I was quite young, I've devoted a great deal of energy to daydreaming. My family remembers me as a quiet child, somewhat withdrawn, determined, and not a little obstinate. I remember that I always found it easy to invent games outdoors and that it was more fun to climb the huge chestnut tree in the yard than to play with dolls. My games were often different from those usually associated with "nice little girls." A playful uncle who wasn't much older than me and the boys up the road always let me join them in building forts, playing cowboys and Indians, or engaging in other make-believe activities. In short, I was a bit of a tomboy.

At the same time, my interest in the great white open spaces of the world grew out of the stories I heard as a child and the books I read when I grew older. The first dream of exploration I remember was as a six-year-old, one about my own expedition. I had been to the cinema with my father to see the documentary of Thor Heyerdahl's *Kon-Tiki* expedition of 1947. I think I had mixed the movie with a Norwegian song about children from around the world. My plan as a six-year-old was to travel on all the oceans and meet kids from all over the globe. I also recall what I thought I should bring as food on my expedition: all kinds of chocolate, cake, and the goodies I loved that my parents only let us have on Saturdays. I don't recall whether I had thought at all about bringing fresh water. The following year, on a trip overseas with my family, I experienced seasickness for the first time, killing the dream of my first expedition.

Later, when I was in fifth grade, my class watched the *Kon-Tiki* documentary, and I recalled my old dream. The documentary was nothing like I remembered, and I started to read about and follow Thor Heyerdahl's projects. Today, I am a board member of the Thor Heyerdahl Institute, and in 2015 I joined a scientific expedition that planned to go from Peru to Easter Island and on south and then drift back to Chile. I was on the raft starting from Easter Island, until we were rescued by the Chilean Armada when the ropes holding together the balsa logs started to rot. We spent seventy-two days on the Pacific on the raft, without seeing a ship. I read thirty books in that time, and I loved my watches under the starry nights. My childhood dream had come true.

Reading about great feats and tragedies in the Arctic and Antarctic had already become a burning interest for me when I was a child. And the older I grew, the more interesting I found these books about Scott, Nansen, and Shackleton. Gradually, I began to understand that those old characters were just like the rest of us when it came to describing an expedition—and the more participants involved in an expedition, the more versions available about what really happened. After the first official reports and diaries of expedition leaders had been published, the original records and those of other participants eventually became available, too.

Amundsen was rather diplomatic when he described the drama that unfolded at his Antarctic base at Framheim after the abortive start for the South Pole in September 1911. Scott couldn't bring himself to admit that he'd made any mistakes, even during the last days of his life with his dead companions beside him. Doubts still hang over Admiral Byrd's flights, supposedly the first of their kind, to the North and South Poles. As the

At age six, with a *Kon-Tiki* raft

years pass, more sources are uncovered, and we continually have more answers as to what really happened. As with all history, it's this unraveling that makes polar history so fascinating.

When I was eight years old, my father, a builder, had to do some maintenance work at Polhøgda, Fridtjof Nansen's home at Lysaker, outside Oslo, and I accompanied him. Compared to other countries, Norway doesn't have many historical buildings, but Polhøgda is one of them. Likewise, Nansen is our national hero, and it's perhaps characteristic that he was neither a soldier nor a political leader but a skiing pioneer and the founder of modern polar exploration, in that order.

On that first visit to Polhøgda, we were shown around, and what fixed itself especially in my memory was seeing Nansen's study in the tower, the leading feature of the building. I remember the desk, chair, pens, and picture of Nansen's wife, Eva, an accomplished singer who gave some of Edvard Grieg's compositions their first performance, dressed for the concert stage. Everything was as Nansen had left it when he died in May 1930 of a heart attack.

In that room, events played out that have virtually become part of Norwegian folklore. There, one day in 1907, Nansen sat on the horns of a dilemma as he waited for Roald Amundsen to arrive. Nansen was to give Amundsen an answer to his request for the loan of *Fram*, the ship that Nansen had specially built for his historic Arctic drift of 1893–96. Amundsen wanted to make an attempt on the North Pole; Nansen had designs on the South Pole. On his way down to receive Amundsen, Nansen passed Eva in the gallery, and she said, "I know very well what you have decided." That persuaded Nansen to change his mind. He descended the last few steps and received Amundsen with the words, "You shall have *Fram*."

Meanwhile, in 1909, Frederick Cook and Robert E. Peary returned from the Arctic, both claiming to have reached the North Pole. (Cook was later unmasked as a fraud, and to this day it's a matter of dispute whether Peary actually reached the Pole.) At that point, Amundsen had decided in all secrecy to turn around and make for the South Pole instead. It is part of the story that Nansen, having been intimately involved in the (bloodless) achievement of Norwegian independence from Sweden in 1905, looked forward to another polar expedition. He wrote to Amundsen after Amundsen returned from the Antarctic having won the race for the South Pole in December 1911:

> I have really done my best for you and your expedition; I can say what you perhaps have not understood, that I have made a greater sacrifice for you than for any other living person, in that I gave up my expedition to the South Pole, the crown of my work as a polar explorer, and renounced Fram so that you could carry out your drift over the Polar Sea. You might think that was not much; but you might consider that it was a plan that I had already considered before sailing on Fram, and which I had planned in all its detail in the hut on Franz Josef's Land.

Returning home from my visit to Polhøgda, I immediately started to read Nansen's book *The First Crossing of Greenland*. His Greenland expedition was the historic opening of modern polar exploration, but the book's old Danish-Norwegian literary language was probably a little heavy for an eight-year-old. The next day, I got hold instead of a school edition of Amundsen's account of his expedition to the South Pole. I drank in every word and, doubtless from that moment, felt a kind of attraction to the far horizons, solitude, cold, and elements.

In addition to Amundsen's description of the ski tour to the South Pole, what particularly fascinated me in his book was the building of the base at Framheim. The stores and workshops under the snow and all the details of equipment made for exciting reading. It was all about preparation and execution down to the tiniest detail. But I think what most attracted me to Amundsen's story was the idea of being *underway* for so long. It meant being alone and independent with everything that you need: tent,

My deep reading of polar literature helped make me both physically and mentally prepared. Photograph by Einar Glestad.

food, sleeping bag, cookstove, and fuel. It meant being able to manage with simple means. Much later, I was able to give this a name: a sense of freedom.

After this literary experience, I began my expedition life through books. Like other teenage girls, I also read what were considered "girls' stories," but I thought that polar literature was much more interesting. I was always hunting for books about girls who had done something similar. Once I found a book called *Amor on Skis*. That was before I knew who "Amor" really was—the Norwegian version of Cupid; but "a'mor" is also slang for "a mother," so I thought the book was about a mother on skis. It turned out to be about girls falling like ninepins as soon as a good-looking boy appeared on the slopes. That book was my first, and greatest, literary disappointment.

FINDING MY OWN WAY

Many years later, when I was thirty years old, it was like seeing the light when I read in the newspaper about Carl Emil Petersen, whose solo ski tour across Greenland in 1983 sounded splendid—and he was fifty-eight years old, to boot. It was a revelation. Carl Emil was a seasoned traveler, but I knew I was also a reliable skier with plenty of stamina.

Why couldn't I also ski across Greenland?

I remember that day so well. I was sitting at the kitchen table with a cup of coffee and the local paper in front of me. My partner sat directly opposite me, immersed in local news, but I was already on my way across Greenland. I was bubbling over with enthusiasm. How could I have ignored the classic route across Greenland and only walked around dreaming of following in Amundsen's footsteps to the South Pole? Whom could I persuade to accompany me? My partner didn't even look up. He had no taste for camping and was definitely not fired up by the thought of an expedition of this kind.

During the days that followed, it was as if I was possessed by Greenland. The more interest I showed in the project, the quieter my partner became. As the weeks passed, he began to understand that my dream would become reality, and not long after I found myself alone—again.

This was nothing new. My taste for advanced outdoor activities and an independent life had always been an obstacle in previous relationships, because it often introduced an element of competition. It was perfectly acceptable, if not entirely legitimate, that the men in my life had stimulating interests, but when I sought the same stimulation, they regarded me as a competitor. The majority of them disliked competition. It was never my intention to defeat them in time or distance; I merely felt that I had the same right to test myself. I couldn't help being physically strong.

To make things more difficult, I didn't have typical "feminine" interests. The other wives and girlfriends didn't clamber up mountain faces, and so at parties I always found myself in the men's corner. Naturally, I was expected to stay with the ladies and stick to fashion, interior decoration, and child-rearing. I did try. Luckily, as time passed, there were more and more women with outdoor interests who found it rewarding to discuss things other than homemaking, but for some years I really felt like an outsider.

Most of my female friends eventually married, had children, and settled down. For many years, I felt a certain pressure, on the part of both parents and friends, to do the same. But at an early age I understood that it would be difficult to find a place in my life for children of my own.

I've always panicked if the days resemble each other. I seem to fall into a comatose state if I have to do the same thing again and again. Everyone told me that if only I had children, this discontent would disappear. Naturally, I was doubtful, but thought that people don't experiment with having children.

The pleasures of family life are undoubtedly many, but for some people the responsibilities and difficulties of realizing ambitions add up to a reality that can be hard to live with. From the outside, family life seemed idyllic, but gradually I learned about its frustrations. As a high school teacher of literature and sports, I became acquainted with another, less attractive, side of family life. It's not easy to be young when your parents are more concerned with their careers and an active social life than with their children.

There has often been a man in my life, but as soon as talk of marriage and children came up, I felt something like claustrophobia and ended the relationship. It gradually became clear that a state of dependence did not exactly suit me. All the fine words about "mutual respect" and "a desire for fulfilment within the relationship" were easy to subscribe to during the early stages. Reality, however, was often completely different.

Norway has been at the vanguard of equality between the sexes—in theory, at least. For many, the practice has been different, both in the home and at work. Most opportunities have gradually become open to women, but we have been expected to carry out the same domestic duties allotted to women for decades while at the same time coping with the demands of a job. Ancient attitudes persist in both sexes. Our generation has obviously seen much success on the road to emancipation, but many women face the reality of having to work two jobs—and often uphill.

I have had to harden myself in various ways and learn to flout other people's expectations when my own goal seemed important enough. In fact, I started on my really good trips only during periods of being alone or, as things are now, when I have found an unusually supportive and mature man.

Fortunately, as time passed, it became clear that when all was said and done, if my goal meant enough to me, the loss of a partner wasn't the worst that could happen.

A FIRST TEST IN GREENLAND

The dream of crossing Greenland wouldn't relax its grip, but finding companions turned out to be much harder than I had expected. None of the men I knew to be capable of the enterprise were particularly keen on having female company. It would have to be women only, but even that wasn't as easy as it seemed. The fit women I knew from athletics thought that the challenge was intriguing, but they couldn't imagine doing without a shower. The thought of crawling into a cold, windblown tent after a long day's march tempted none of my female friends. Nor were the few whom I knew from climbing prepared for an all-women expedition: ought we not to include a man—or two?

The woman who finally accepted the challenge, and ultimately became a marvelous expedition companion, was Julie Maske. I first met her on Svalbard in 1989, where I had spent one month the previous two summers guiding trekking tours and ski expeditions. Julie, too, spent the summer months up there as a travel guide, and I had heard that she was a fine, tough woman. I was leaving the quay at Longyearbyen on one boat, while Julie was arriving on another. We greeted each other, and I called over to her, "Will you come with me to ski across Greenland?"

"Yes!" I heard, as the boats drew away from each other. That's the way, I thought—it will be all right with her.

Eventually we found two more women and started from

eastern Greenland in April 1991. Due to storms, we had to wait twelve days before the helicopter was able to take us over the Sermilik Fjord at Ammassalik. We started from the Hahn Glacier in Johan Petersen's Fjord, each hauling a sled weighing ninety kilos (about 200 pounds).

After only three days, we were overtaken by a *pitarq*, the Eskimo word for the violent katabatic wind that sweeps without warning down the glacier with hurricane force. It's not often that one experiences a hurricane out in the open, and only those who have done so know what it means. We didn't have a hope of pitching our tent but instead moved the contents of two of the sleds into the other two and lay down back-to-back in the empty sleds.

At a certain point, I had the impression that the wind was easing, and I wanted to secure the sleds with snow anchors. I raised myself a little to listen to the wind. There came a violent roar, and I was lifted up and flung down brutally on my back. It knocked the breath out of me. I had to struggle to control my breathing and my rising panic and try to raise myself up again. The wind and driving snow knocked the breath out of me once more. Nothing was visible, just a mass of white. The snow was driving into my anorak and up my back. My elbows and knees were already wet, and I was cold. The rising temperature had made the snow wet. Carefully, I raised myself and looked up again, and through the driving snow I glimpsed the red covers on the sleds where the others were sitting. I crawled back the ten meters to them.

After seventeen hours bivouacked in the sleds, while the storm tore at us and at our equipment, the wind dropped, and we discovered a fuel leak. Some of our food was swimming in gasoline. We decided to change course. The plan was to follow the route that Nansen originally intended, from "the bottom of the long Sermilik Fjord . . . to climb up onto the icecap" and cross over to Disko Bay on the west coast.

But the pitarq did not turn out to be our only setback. The

Primus stoves soon began to fail. Cleaning didn't help at all. Eventually, we figured out that the gasoline was leaded, even though we had ordered unleaded. (After returning home, we had the stoves tested and found that the tubes were indeed clogged with lead.)

Finally, one day up on the heights, it was absolutely impossible to get any sign of life out of the Primus stoves. The temperature was –35 degrees Celsius (–31 degrees Fahrenheit); we had no chance of melting snow or cooking warm food. A pleasing prospect!

We activated our emergency transmitter, making contact with an aircraft, and told the pilot our woeful tale of fuel in our food and Primus stoves that refused to work. New stoves and fuel and a couple of hundred kilos of tinned food arrived by airdrop. The police on board the aircraft overhead also gave us orders to turn back, both verbally and, for good measure, written. They came from Godthaab. I cited the instructions that had been issued by the police in the town of Tasiilaq before we started. Whatever happened, we were to continue westward. They didn't have helicopters capable of rescuing us.

We four women agreed that we had now received all the help we needed. We were in good shape. Instead of turning back, we would go to the abandoned American base DYE 2 in the middle of the icecap and then continue to Søndre Strømfjord on the west coast. If we heard aircraft, we would transmit our position and report how we were faring. We packed up and continued westward. I had an uneasy feeling that defying the orders of the police chief would not be well received in Godthaab. I considered letting the radio batteries drain so that we couldn't make contact with any aircraft. But something might happen again, so I didn't pursue that idea.

By now, we had come so far to the west that the katabatic wind from the icecap started helping us on our way. We began sailing with our Up-Skis—big parachutes that can be opened in the middle. If it blew too hard, we could open them a little to reduce speed. To stop, we opened them completely. It's a wonderful feeling to be carried along on skis by the wind.

One day, after making good progress for some time, we heard the sound of an aircraft close by. We called it on our radio to give our position and report that all was well. In reply, we received a message from the police chief in Godthaab, relayed by the pilot: "If you continue, your expedition permit will be withdrawn. In that case, your insurance, which is conditional on the permit, will be invalid."

To me, that message was like a body blow. Afterward I heard what had happened: the police chief had been at a bar, half-drunk, and declared that he would "get those females off the glacier." He had no right to do what he did. Discussing the message we had received, two of us wanted to carry on; two wanted to turn back. According to Julie, I cried for twenty seconds before resigning myself to the inevitable and abandoning our goal. We swung compass and skis in the opposite direction, turned back, and started retracing our tracks to the east.

After a day in the same tracks, we agreed to manage on our own. We would not go down to the Hahn Glacier and wait there for a helicopter. Instead, we'd go right down to the little hunting settlement at Isotorq and send our equipment home by boat. If we were to be fetched by helicopter, we would be unable to take any of our equipment. The police and rescue service would subsequently retrieve it and sell it. In fact, the authorities in Ammassalik had offered to sell us abandoned equipment. Three other expeditions had had to be rescued during that storm-filled spring. Our equipment was worth just as much to us as it was to the police in Greenland.

We had heard that there were good routes down the glacier to Isotorq. Our small-scale maps (1:1,000,000) were anything but ideal, but with good visibility and satellite navigation that fixed our position to within fifteen meters (fifty feet), we felt we would manage. We never did have proper visibility, but we felt our way down the glacier by lunging forward with our ski poles to detect possible crevasses or icefalls. We also tried to follow the lateral moraine. On the way down, we had another pitarq, but this time the tent was already pitched, and the moraine gave a little shelter.

At home, meanwhile, family and friends were worried. Because of bad weather, the return journey took longer than expected, and we made no further radio contact. On the basis of earlier contacts, the press had decided that things were not going well with the girls out on their ski tour. Front-page headlines about storms, no food, and fuel leaks hardly reassured our families.

On the eve of May 17, Norway's Constitution Day, we were down by the fjord at last. We woke up that day to brilliant sunshine. It's hard to convey to an outsider the significance of Constitution Day (called *syttende mai* by Norwegians). The country achieved independence from Sweden only in 1905, but May 17 commemorates the adoption in 1814 of the present Norwegian Constitution and the first step toward national sovereignty. If you imagine a combination of Bastille Day and the Fourth of July, but stripped of military overtones, you'll have some idea of the emotions involved. Our polar explorers, for example, always celebrated Constitution Day, no matter the circumstances.

We were certainly not going to break that tradition. We fired a salute with emergency rockets and sang a patriotic song. Historical considerations aside, we were pleased to be down safely from the glacier, and, what was more, the fjord was still safely frozen over.

A Greenland hunter heard the noise we were making and came along to investigate. With his dog team, he hauled our sleds back to Isortoq. That same evening, we were able to call home and report that we were safely down from the glacier. We had been on the icecap for twenty-eight days, twenty of which were in whiteout and blizzard conditions.

The expedition had not been what Julie and I had hoped. On the way home, we were already beginning to discuss a new one for the following year.

SKIING AGAINST
THE TIDE

The expedition to Greenland hadn't exactly been a gold mine, but at least we had acquired equipment and experience. Even having seen the worst side of the icecap was no consolation for defeat. Turning back had been a bitter experience, and we looked forward to trying again. The next year, at the beginning of May, we flew to Søndre Strømfjord. Only our families and our closest friends knew that we had gone there.

Most who cross the Greenland icecap do so from east to west, partly due to historical reasons. Nansen made his celebrated first crossing in that direction, but in his day the east coast was sparsely populated, there were no European settlements, and communication with the outside world was virtually nonexistent. On the west coast, by contrast, there were several Danish colonies, with regular ships plying between Greenland and Europe.

Another reason for crossing Greenland from east to west is that travelers are helped by the katabatic winds blowing in that direction. There are disadvantages, however, like unstable weather. Also, the Sermilik Fjord hadn't frozen over in recent years. Whether people start from Isortoq or Ammasalik (Tasilaq), this means depending on helicopters to cross the fjord and reach the glacier tongues leading up to the icecap. Since we had had to wait twelve days both for transport and for good weather the previous year, this time Julie and I had agreed to swim against the tide. We decided to start from the airfield at Søndre Strøm-fjord on the west coast and ski eastward to Isortoq, accepting the burden of extra headwind.

We sent the sleds in advance, almost ready packed. The year before we had learned that good progress over *sastrugi* (long, wavelike ridges of snow, formed by the wind on the polar plains) and through loose snow was impossible while dragging heavy sleds. We managed to pare down the loads to fifty kilos (110 pounds). We had food for twenty-five days, plus some emergency rations. That meant we had to cover an average of twenty-three kilometers (about fourteen miles) every single day.

This is all very well if we were planning to ski in Nordmarka, the local terrain around my home in Oslo. But our previous ex-cursion to Greenland had taught us that blizzards and sastrugi mean that skiing in those conditions can't be compared with a tour over well-prepared domestic tracks. We were prepared for hard going, and therefore didn't delay our start.

Only three hours after landing at Søndre Strømfjord, we were on our way to begin the climb toward Point 660 at the end of the Sandflugt Valley. This point lies like an island in the ice. It is the goal of everyone coming down the icecap when crossing from east to west and the starting point for those going in the opposite direction. It's the easiest place to leave or enter the ice-cap. On either side of the point are giant seracs (chunks of ice) and huge crevasses.

Seven hours after starting, we got our first glimpse of the ice-fall. Glinting in the evening sun, the seracs seemed to stretch out mile after mile. The sight gave us butterflies by the thousand in our stomachs, and we felt a combination of intense pleasure and great excitement. It looked as if threading our way through the moraine and up the icefall was going to be an interminable task.

Having identified Point 660, we made camp. We crept into our sleeping bags scarcely twenty-two hours after breakfast at home in Oslo. In that space of time we had been catapulted from a Norwegian spring morning and 20 degrees Celsius (68 degrees Fahrenheit) in the shade to a Greenland spring evening and −30 degrees Celsius (−22 degrees Fahrenheit). We had a proper map and knew what lay ahead. This knowledge, together with the fact that we had reached our starting point so quickly, reminded us that, compared with Nansen (against whom we always instinctively measured ourselves), we were merely on a ski tour. He had been on an expedition.

Beyond sheer drudgery, traversing the icefall posed no problems. After three days, we were able to remove the skins on our skis and use wax instead. Thereafter, we could glide ahead, which is the joy of skiing, rather than plod, which is its bane.

Both Julie and I like this kind of vacation. We enjoy traveling with all our necessities packed in a sled and a rucksack and all decisions in our control. Division of labor is automatic and instinctive. One of us cooks dinner and breakfast inside the tent, while the other secures everything outside against the wind in the evening or, in the morning, digs out the sleds and waxes them. Happiness is when the Primus is roaring, we're well fed, and we're pleased with the day's work. There's nothing more pleasurable than tent life, even on mornings when, with a temperature of −38 degrees Celsius (−36 degrees Fahrenheit) outside, you need a little extra determination to creep out of your sleeping bag.

One day we were stormbound and entertained ourselves in the tent by reading aloud from a biography of the Greenland explorer Knud Rasmussen. One hundred kilometers (sixty-two miles) from Isortoq, we were overtaken by an unbelievable snowfall: 1 meter 40 centimeters (about four and a half feet) in the course of a day and a night. The sleds were snowed under and had capsized. We simply had to lie still and wait for the wind to pack the snow while we took turns digging out the tent. After that snowfall, we counted on an extra week on the icecap and

With Julie Maske near the east coast of the Greenland icecap after our crossing in 1992.

had already calculated new rations when the wind began to blow. It was a proper storm, with sleet, thunder, and lightning, which kept us tent-bound for yet another day. In our little igloo tent, which stood out like a lightning rod on the inland ice, we went through nerve-racking moments while the thunderstorm passed over us. We devoutly hoped that the skis outside stuck up higher than the tent.

The following day the surface was packed as hard as agate by the storm. It was easy to ski, and we covered the last hundred kilometers in two days. The highest point of the icecap was at an altitude of 2,500 meters (about 8,000 feet), but we didn't have a sensation of going downhill before the afternoon of the last day. That was the best day of the entire ski tour.

We hadn't seen the sun for five days, but that afternoon it broke through the clouds just before we caught a glimpse of the first nunataks (rock pinnacles sticking out of the ice) and we were able to make our first double heaves on the ski poles. That final afternoon was like a fairy tale: sunset and evening breeze in a long downhill run that lasted three hours. To the left and right were nunataks, and ahead was the sea with hundreds of icebergs. Pleasure spread throughout our bodies, and calm descended on us. That was happiness indeed! Whether it was speed or emotion that made the tears run, I have no idea, but there is something sacred about moments such as these.

We had covered 570 kilometers (355 miles) in twenty-three days. At this stage of the game, if adventurers are to distinguish their own efforts from those who went before, it is necessary to contrive a new variation on the old familiar theme. In our case, we were the first women to cross from one side of the inland ice to the other unsupported and without dogs.

Life on the great white open spaces is wonderful, and I remember that at that moment my thoughts flew to an icecap even bigger than the one we had just crossed.

MY PROVOCATIVE
ANNOUNCEMENT

It's not easy to find skiing companions who are both physically and mentally strong. Until Julie decided to join me, I had toyed with the idea of sneaking across Greenland alone, even though it was no longer officially allowed. Carl Emil Petersen was the last to cross Greenland alone—at least the last with official sanction.

When we finally crossed Greenland, Julie had said that, unlike me, she was finished with the great white open spaces. She would not be coming with me to the South Pole. That was a setback. One has to be extremely careful in choosing companions for such an enterprise. Three weeks after returning home from Greenland, I heard that Erling Kagge was planning to go to the South Pole alone. That was not prohibited, which gave me something to think about. Perhaps the only way of skiing to the South Pole was to do it solo.

During the next few days, that thought refused to go away. I raised the subject one evening, to the unmistakable amusement of my husband, Einar, and some friends I was with. It hadn't even been a month since I had returned from Greenland, and they thought I was joking.

I had rarely been more serious. I followed Erling's expedition with great attention, and I discussed my plans with Sjur Mørdre, who had been to both the North and South Poles besides having crossed Greenland on several occasions. He's always ready to share his experience with others.

I contacted Erling when he returned home. I was most concerned about the crevassed areas, because it's always riskier to travel alone in deeply fissured terrain. Reassured by what he told me, shortly after our conversation I had fully made up my mind.

My family backed me up, though my mother was furious. When was I going to settle down? She didn't speak to me during the whole of the Easter holiday. She was understandably worried. Also, she would rather have seen her nearly forty-year-old daughter pregnant with something other than a plan to ski solo to the South Pole.

My father also expressed concern over my plans, but I pointed out that he had only himself to blame for my attraction to the South Pole. He accepted the argument that it was all due to the stories he used to tell me and to that first childhood visit to Polhøgda.

Einar is in many ways a special kind of man. He isn't troubled by my taste for demanding and dangerous sports. He is an outdoor enthusiast, and we train together all year round, but he avoids vertical mountain walls and weeks on end in a tent in subzero temperatures. But he recently made a dream of his own come true.

After many years as an economist and the director of his own wholesale company, he changed course completely. He had always wanted to be a physiotherapist, but because of the family business, he chose, or was compelled, to study economics instead. One evening some years ago, he sighed and said, "What I admire in you, Liv, is that you realize your plans and dreams." I asked him what was preventing him from doing the same. A year or two later he was a student again. Now he's a qualified physiotherapist.

When we first began to discuss moving in together in 1986, I made it clear that I had no intention of filling a traditional house-wife's role. Two or three times a week I went straight from my teaching job to my other work as a Nordic ski-racing coach. I spent many weekends working at training camps or officiating at races. I wanted to continue with all of this. During a large part of my summer vacations I also wanted to continue working as a travel guide on Svalbard, and Einar knew all about my Greenland plans. He saw no difficulty with my choices.

This was a thoroughly unfamiliar attitude on the part of a man, and my feelings for Einar did not cool. For the first time I wasn't condemned for having chosen a way of life a little out of the ordinary. It was an ideal foundation on which to build a good life together. The division of labor was simple: each looked after his or her own. If one or the other thought the house was too untidy to have guests, then that person would simply clean up. We agreed that it was better to be a little messy and comfort-able than to concentrate fanatically on a spotless model home. I cooked my first dinner after we had been living together for a year. It was received as if it were Christmas Eve and everyone's birthdays all at the same time. Now we have a reasonably fair division of domestic duties—and it's still somewhat untidy.

I met Einar and his previous wife through a Nordic ski-racing group in a suburb of Oslo. We trained together, and a few couples met regularly to sing ballads, a rather Norwegian form of conviviality. In 1985 Einar's wife died suddenly from heart failure caused by asthma. Einar was left alone with three daughters: Jan-nicke, Linn, and Birgitte, then fourteen, eleven, and six years old.

At the time, I was emerging from a failed relationship and had applied for a year's leave from my school to work as a ski instructor in Australia. Unfortunately, I couldn't get a work per-mit, so I began taking a postgraduate course at the Norwegian School of Sport Sciences in Oslo instead, while I also worked as a teacher and leisure supervisor at a collective for drug addicts. I wanted to study a combination of physical training and mental health.

The collective had just been established, and the staff had to be trained. Few had any experience in youth work, and the encounter with these deeply disturbed youngsters was too trying for most. One by one the others gave notice. It was impossible to keep proper shifts, and finally the work kept me fully occupied. I didn't have the energy to complete my postgraduate course.

The youngsters in the collective had endured a hard up-bringing and had experienced things that I had hitherto only read about in the tabloid press. Yet they were resourceful, even if they had had a difficult start. They needed me, and I gave them all I had. I worked so hard that in the end I was completely exhausted. Family and friends pointed out that this couldn't go on, and eventually even I recognized that no one was gaining from my being on the verge of collapse. Finally, I quit and bought an airplane ticket to Katmandu in the spring of 1985. I wanted to visit the Himalayas, another dream of mine.

HARDENING MYSELF IN
THE HIMALAYAS

In Katmandu I met up with Nora, a friend from Oslo who had also chosen an unconventional lifestyle. She was going to the Mount Everest Base Camp in the Khumbu Valley as a travel guide for a party of tourists, and I joined them for several days.

In the Khumbu Valley, I discovered what altitude sickness means. I also saw and heard about its tragic consequences. After a few days, I left Nora's group and found a party of Frenchmen, to whom I attached myself. We had all been up to base camp, and my new friends wanted to climb a 5,600-meter peak (about 18,000 feet high). I had a headache and felt it would be sensible to rest, but a sprightly sixty-year-old lady from Texas also wanted to climb that mountain; she wanted company and persuaded me to go with her.

There would be no difficulty keeping up with her, I thought. As soon as the terrain got steep, however, I had difficulty breathing. My new American climbing companion had been in Nepal for two months and was therefore acclimated. I had just fled from a job, completely worn out, and had rushed up to the heights, so I was far from acclimatized. While I needed all my energy merely to advance ten paces without stopping, the Texan lady was chattering away. At first, I could at least manage a *yes* or *no*, but finally it was all I could do to breathe. My head was aching, I was giddy, and I had to go down on all fours every ten steps to rest and catch my breath. But I did reach the top.

That night we were to sleep in a hut at an altitude of 5,500 meters. I awoke in the middle of the night with a horrible thirst, breathing difficulties, and a frightful headache. The water bottle was frozen solid. One of my French acquaintances was in the same condition. Deciding then and there to go back down to the valley, we stumbled down a drop in altitude of a thousand meters (3,250 feet) in the moonlight to the plateau where the village of Pheriche lies. Conditions were totally different there, and had I been asked if I was in a fit enough state to run a marathon, my answer would have been yes. At the hospital they said that it had been a tragic week in the Khumbu Valley. Six people had died of altitude sickness, one of the complications of which is hydrocephalus, or water on the brain. This is caused by a difference in pressure in the tissues, which is precipitated by a sudden drop in atmospheric pressure.

From Lukla, I flew to Katmandu, where I had arranged to meet Nora again. In Katmandu, I also met for the first time Ulf Prytz, who would later became my boss at Svalbard Polar Travel. They were both going to Lhasa, in Tibet, to investigate the possibilities of arranging tours. Tibet had fascinated me ever since primary school, when my class had taken part in a campaign to help Tibetan schoolchildren suffering the effects of Chinese oppression. I, too, wanted to go on to Tibet.

The others had visas, but I didn't. Visas were supposedly hard to get, and many people had waited weeks for one. Oddly enough, in my case everything went smoothly. At the Chinese consulate, my little red Norwegian passport was received with broad smiles. I was told that if I had a photograph, I could have a visa immediately. Two hours later I had a Chinese visa, having sacrificed the picture from my driver's license.

Mother of the World, as it is called on this side—took our breath away. It rose up in lonely majesty, shimmering white against the blazing blue sky. I was strongly drawn to the mountain and would have loved to be one of the climbers in base camp. In the Khumbu Valley, on the other side of Everest, I had met Edmund Hillary, who was there building a school and who in 1953, together with the Sherpa Tenzing Norgay, had been the first to reach the summit.

Perhaps one day it would be my turn.

"HAVE YOU EVER HAULED A SLED, MY DEAR?"

After three months in Nepal and Tibet, I was home again. Einar came courting. Before autumn was over we were living together, and after a couple of years we married. At last I had found a man who encouraged me instead of holding me back. The time had come to realize my plan to ski to the South Pole.

To get within striking distance of southern latitudes, I had to begin with money, the cornerstone of any expedition. I had a little brochure printed in Norwegian and English with my choice of route and other practical information. With my head held high and a wildly beating heart, I went to my first meeting with a potential sponsor. I had deliberately chosen Lill-Sport, a Norwegian manufacturer of rucksacks and sportswear, because I knew them to be favorably inclined. The outcome heartened me to carry on.

The weeks that followed were less encouraging. After the first few meetings, I was left with the distinct impression that it was generally considered unnatural for a woman to willingly expose herself to fifty days of isolation in the frozen wastes. When my interrogators grasped that I proposed to haul a sled weighing a hundred kilos (220 pounds), they stared at me across their desks in disbelief, plainly regarding me as an unrealistic dreamer.

The hunt for sponsors turned out to be much harder than I had imagined. Their reactions indicated that it must have been considerably more difficult for me than for the men who had made the rounds before me. "Have you ever hauled a sled?" was a constantly recurring question. I wondered if the same question had been put to the boys. Certainly, they didn't have to sit through all the stories of military service. In the end, I had heard enough tales of winter maneuvers to fill a book. Having been told all those dramatic episodes, I could only marvel at how many Norwegians survive military service in winter.

I was taken aback by these reactions. I had sensed them in private life for many years, but I believed that contemporary manufacturers were more tolerant and open-minded. In Norway, our prime minister at the time was (and is now) a woman, and we have many female politicians and cabinet ministers, as well as women in the armed forces and most of the professions. Business and industry actively encourage women, don't they? My generation is one of transition, in which everything has been fundamentally open to all. Nonetheless, often something or someone is holding us back. Was I intruding on something that belonged to men alone? Were the poles of the earth their last refuge?

I talked to some leaders in industry about sponsorship but was unequivocally rejected. Even women in top positions barricaded themselves behind subordinates and were completely inaccessible. Eventually, I understood that planning an expedition to the South Pole was treading on male preserves. Women don't go to the South Pole—at least not alone.

I had faced obstacles in my outdoor life before, but I hadn't given up easily. It wasn't until 1976 that women were allowed to enter the Birkebeinerrennet. This is a cross-country ski race of fifty-five kilometers (thirty-five miles) over a mountain range, in which skiers carry a rucksack that originally weighed five and a half kilos (twelve pounds) but has now been reduced to three and a half kilos (eight pounds). I skied in the first Birkebeinerrennet for women and remember well the reaction when I overtook one of the old veterans snowplowing and pole riding down a slope. He gave way but hit me on the neck with one of his ski poles, shouting, "Bloody woman!" I was sore where he hit me for more than a month.

Men have always had a monopoly on polar expeditions. When it was finally my turn, there was a feeling that such undertakings by women were too much of a good thing. Very few applauded a forty-year-old woman who wanted to extend the frontiers a little.

What really helped was when someone who knew me through sports could open doors. I sold the project as best I could. Luckily, there was no doubt that it was a matter of selling, not begging (though neither is particularly easy). Those companies that contribute to such an expedition do so because of what they believe they can get in return. Some see an opportunity to develop and market their products, while others consider it a means of inspiring their employees. With very few exceptions, nobody simply donates money now without an expectation of something in return. I did, however, receive a few checks from private individuals wishing me good luck. This was encouraging because it showed that at least some people believed in me. A few no doubt thought that I deserved a chance, even though I always had the feeling they didn't believe that, as a woman, I could really be expected to succeed. In any case, it was a long way from goodwill to solid finance.

After a lot of effort and many meetings, I finally secured several declarations of intent. At that point the Aurora expedition (a Norwegian effort, led by Monica Kristensen, to find the tent left by Amundsen at the South Pole) had a fatal accident in Antarctica. One of the members was killed in a crevasse. That the leader was a woman didn't help matters. As a direct result of the accident, my own sponsors became frightened, and many of my hard-won declarations of intent, totaling £50,000 (about $75,000), were withdrawn. I was supposed to set off in barely a year. I virtually had to begin all over again.

A hard time followed, and it would have been simplest to give up. But something within me refused to do so; that would have been letting myself down. My goal was so clear that I refused to be stopped by the lack of some miserable cash. Einar and some good friends cheered me on.

Luckily, I was in the right place at the right time for once. International Sector Sport Watches, a Swiss company, and No Limits Techware, an Italian sports apparel company, heard about my project. They thought it was unique and decided to be main sponsors.

Compared with foreign manufacturers, Norwegian suppliers and consumers have one great advantage. Abroad, mass markets and long production runs hinder modification. In Norway, on the other hand, with a small population and proportionally small markets, production runs are shorter, and changes can be made with comparative ease and speed. For this reason, much Norwegian-made equipment has attained extremely high quality. With the exception of a custom-made belt on my rucksack, everything I used on my expedition could be bought in Norwegian sports shops. In the end, I looked like a Christmas tree, with my anorak, trousers, sled, and cap covered in corporate logos.

The old polar pioneers weren't similarly decked out, but they had their sponsors, too. While there were still blank spaces on the map, royalty and businessmen considered it an honor to support polar expeditions. In this way they secured immortality by having newly discovered fjords, mountains, glaciers, and such named after them.

Insurance turned out to be unexpectedly difficult and expensive. Unfortunately for me, Lloyd's of London had had to pay out a large sum to Sir Ranulph Fiennes and Mike Stroud, who had tried to cross Antarctica, man-hauling and unsupported all the way from Berkner Island to the American base at McMurdo Sound. All things considered, it's amazing that they came as far as they did—right down to the Ross Ice Shelf at the foot of the Beardmore Glacier, more dead than alive—before activating their emergency transmitter. Fiennes had been running expeditions for twenty years, but nonetheless "learning by doing" seemed an alien concept to him. In England he's something of a hero—perhaps because he's gotten himself into difficulties so often? Their planning must have been fundamentally flawed. They froze horribly along the way. Soon after starting, before they had reached the plateau, they thought their sleds were too heavy, so to save weight they jettisoned their down jackets! Lloyd's was understandably disillusioned. Under similar circumstances, what could they expect of a woman? Underwriters weren't exactly lining up to accept my risk.

Eventually, an insurance company issued a policy on the condition that I guaranteed a personal excess of £55,000 (about $80,000). This was to secure a Search and Rescue Guarantee of £200,000 ($290,000). It was required by Adventure Network International (ANI), the only private airline serving the Antarctic continent, as an absolute condition of its flying me there. ANI was also going to take me to the starting point on the ice shelf by snowmobile and fly me out from the South Pole. And if I met difficulties along the way, ANI would pick me up.

Antarctic transport was decidedly the most expensive item in my budget. In any case, it was the cheapest Antarctic expedition to date. The estimated cost was $145,000, of which $80,000 was my personal excess under the insurance policy. Nonetheless, I had to suffer various pointed remarks. Some people wondered if I might not have done better to collect money for the care of the aged.

TRAINING WITH TIRES
AND PAVAROTTI

Once my intentions became known, there was no lack of gratuitous commentary. Some people thought my expedition was a lot of nonsense; others expressed their encouragement. Those who knew me were hardly surprised that at last I was going to the South Pole.

I've never stopped playing sports and being active; as I grew older, the urge was channeled more and more into outdoor activities. I started competitive sports at the age of nine. I began with slalom, but when I was thirteen I injured my kneecap, and as a result I was too slow in the gates. I had to find other challenges.

When there's talk of money and sports, I often say to my father that he was well ahead of the game. He literally bribed me to take up cross-country skiing. One day when I was about fourteen, we happened to pass a shop with flame-red cross-country skis in the window. They were highly attractive, and my father said they would be mine if I would take up cross-country ski racing. Since then, it's been my favorite recreation. My mother was, and still is, a good skier, and it was only when I turned seventeen that I was able to keep up with her on long tours in our home terrain of Nordmarka. On winter Sundays, she preferred to come skiing with us rather than stay at home and prepare dinner. We still often go skiing together.

I played handball for some years but found a sport that suited me better when I began orienteering—a cross-country race in which competitors use a map and compass to find their way through unfamiliar terrain. My parents introduced me to orienteering: my mother began to compete together with my younger brother and me, but my father preferred to go off by himself and find a convenient tree stump where he could sit down, light a pipe, and contemplate. I've benefited a great deal from orienteering, which has taken me to places and given me experiences I would otherwise have missed. On one occasion, at a training camp in Valdres, a mountain district north of Oslo, I was putting out checkpoints early one morning. On a bog, I ran into a bear. I felt my hair bristling, and I ran back to the cabin as fast as my legs could carry me. In retrospect, I know that I must be one of the very few people to have seen a bear at close quarters only a few hours from Oslo.

Even though I've now given up serious competitive sports, I still like to take part in ski-touring races and the occasional orienteering run. I'm highly competitive, and I feel the "wild beast" stir within me when I'm waiting at the starting line. Otherwise, if I'm not climbing, kayaking, or working on Svalbard as a mountain guide, I regularly go cycling and jogging. In other words, by any normal standards, I was fit. The ski tour to the South Pole, however, required specialized training.

I prepared myself mentally by imagining that it would be horribly cold, with blizzards most of the way, that it would be extremely difficult to pitch my tent in a storm, and that I'd be frozen to the marrow when I started off each morning. My head was whirling with the fearsome experiences caused by starvation, cold, and poor equipment, which I had read about in polar literature, past and present. Yet despite all the tales of horror, my overriding emotion at the thought of the long ski tour ahead was pleasure. Admittedly, I was worried about the route, whether there would be many crevasses and if progress would be difficult, but I looked forward to setting off. I knew that it would be a hard job hauling a hundred kilos (220 pounds), but I had managed that before, and oddly enough I was looking forward to the grind.

When I started my training, I had only men as standards of comparison, because on previous tours in extreme conditions I had been together with men. These experiences taught me that these men had greater physical strength than I had but that I could match them in physical and mental stamina. Besides, I needed less food. On my return from the South Pole, tests showed that I hadn't lost any muscle fiber, only fat. Under these conditions, men lose muscle as well. I have long legs and great endurance. The longer the distance, whether skiing, running, or cycling, the better I like it. I've never consciously sought out typically male activities, but I have never understood why women shouldn't also take part in trials of stamina.

At the age of seventeen, I'd skied in the Grenaderløp, a cross-country ski race more than ninety kilometers (fifty-six miles) from Hakadal to Asker, outside Oslo. This was before the event was open to women, so to disguise my gender I pulled my cap well down over my forehead. I've cycled in a mass race between Trondheim and Oslo, a distance of 540 kilometers (335 miles), because I like cycling, and I've run in several marathons because the distance suits me. I must have spent at least two years of my life in a tent, and I have eaten innumerable meals cooked on a Primus stove. I have considerable experience with glaciers both on Svalbard and in the mountains of Norway, not to mention blizzards and low temperatures both there and in Greenland.

Nonetheless, even with that experience from my time in Greenland and Svalbard, I lacked the particular qualifications for a successful Antarctic expedition, and I sought advice on where I could find it. There was no need to make the same mistakes others had made before me. The Norwegian polar community is small, and, fortunately, sharing experience with others has become expected. This is different from polar communities in other countries, where anyone going on an expedition is someone else's rival. I won't assert that Norway is entirely free of this phenomenon, but by and large most people are willing to help.

One thing was certain: a ski tour to the South Pole required strength. That in turn meant rigorous training. I love training in general, as long as it means skiing, running, climbing, and so on. But specialized training, of the type required to develop particular groups of muscles, I find to be among the most boring things on earth. Yet, I simply had to strengthen certain muscles: there was no way out. My back is my weak point. If I sit in an office for four days without exercise, the left side of my lower back starts aching.

On Christmas Eve in 1993, the year before reaching the South Pole, I was at home, bedridden with an excruciating backache. It was so bad that I couldn't get out of bed without help. I knew exactly why it was hurting. During a busy period at work, I had done very little training. At the time, I was scheduled to attend a meeting of Svalbard mountain guides at a cabin in Nordmarka, some distance from Oslo. I thought it would be suitable training for me to pull all our food and baggage on a sled, which would require five trips in undulating terrain. With half a meter (twenty inches) of fresh snow, however, it would be too much. An Antarctic explorer could not admit to being incapacitated by backache, so my family received strict instructions to say that I was suffering from influenza.

At first sight, it may seem wholly indefensible even to consider hauling a load weighing a hundred kilos for fifty days with a bad back. But I know my back. My troubles began with immoderate training as a fourteen- and fifteen-year-old athlete. Subsequently, I've never approached the amount of training that I put in as a competitor in girls' cross-country ski racing. At that time there were few qualified trainers, and high-quantity training was popular. The outcome was what today is called overtraining. As a

One of the locals wonders what I am doing dragging tires up the road, but a great many of the people I met showed real interest in the Antarctic. Photograph by Karl Braanaas.

Lommedalen is a popular recreational area, so unless I went out very early, I always met someone when I was dragging my tires. When walkers and cyclists passed by me, they averted their gaze instead of giving the nod that is usual when meeting under such circumstances. I began to understand what it must be like to be an eccentric. After I was featured in press reports, my training rounds became more pleasant. People walked or cycled beside me and talked. It turns out that a surprising number of them admired our old polar heroes. Many confessed that they nursed the same dream as I did but didn't know how to turn it into action. In the end, I felt privileged instead of peculiar when I was hauling my tires. My back had recovered, and I was building up my thigh muscles, as well as my reserves of fat.

On my first expedition to Greenland, I had based my dietary calculations on the energy requirements of a man in the Antarctic, about 6,000 calories daily. Women require fewer calories than men do, but just how much was uncertain. We settled on 5,000, which was far too much and impossible to force down. And after we had gotten gasoline in our food, the true amount of food available was difficult to estimate.

On the second Greenland expedition, based on our own experience, Julie and I decided on 3,900 calories per day. That suited me, even though I couldn't eat it all on this expedition either. I assumed that the same number of calories would do for the South Pole. I consulted nutrition experts, who recommended 4,900 calories per day. In the end I chose 4,200.

Under normal sedentary conditions, a woman needs about 1,800 calories per day for maintenance, a man 2,000. Both require a daily liquid intake of between two and three liters. If one exercises between six and ten times weekly, the figures rise to 3,400 calories for women, 4,000 for men, and between four and six liters of liquid intake. In cold conditions like the Antarctic, one uses more energy to keep warm, and the altitude and rarefied atmosphere of the polar plateau mean that one burns more calories.

An ordinary diet contains about 55–60 percent carbohydrates, 10–15 percent proteins, and 30 percent fat. On expeditions to cold regions, more fat is included because it contains more calories, ounce for ounce, than the other components. This can save many kilos on the sled. My diet in the Antarctic consisted of roughly 44 percent fat, 49 percent carbohydrates, and 7 percent protein. The abdomen is distended after heavy meals, so to avoid feeling hungry I decided to eat little but often.

By putting on ten kilos, I would have considerable reserves to call on. Ten kilos of fat generates about 60,000 calories, which meant 1,000 calories per day. That meant ten kilos less on the sled; and it's easier to carry weight than to haul it behind. I took seven extra daily rations of 1,500 calories each in case I took longer than anticipated or could not obtain food at the South Pole. (This was no academic consideration. For decades the Americans, kilos from my rucksack. It had become impossible to cope with what had hitherto been a manageable load of fifteen kilos on my back and three tires behind me. Now it was a burden to do a couple of hours of training with a reduced load.

It was a wonderful autumn, with fantastic clouds. Even if summer had been Berit's favorite season, I always associated her with autumn. Over the years, we had gone walking in the places where I was now training. We had often discussed life on those occasions, talking a little about the past and dreaming of the future.

Before the summer, she had talked about her new relationship with a mutual colleague. The summer vacation came and went. We managed to meet once or twice but somehow never had time for a proper talk. The last time I saw her was in front of my bank at Bekkestua, near my home. We tried to meet and have a real chat, but both of us were busy. I was preoccupied with my preparations. She thought that my expedition to the South Pole was exciting, but like so many others, she was somewhat doubtful, too. "You're crazy. Get to the South Pole and take the first plane home!" were her last words to me before we went our separate ways.

After the murder, I felt guilty because I had been immersed in my own affairs to the exclusion of all else and hadn't made time to talk to Berit. Somehow I felt responsible for what had happened. Much might have turned out differently had I managed to have a proper talk with her, but perhaps not. Logically, I understood very well that what had happened was not my fault, but when you're in a state of shock and worn out, you don't listen to reason.

I was often overcome by emotion in my training sessions. I began losing the weight I'd been struggling to put on. I felt constantly worn out. I began to wonder if I would be ready in time. Should I postpone the expedition? I had known Berit well;

she would have been furious if she had known what was passing through my mind.

People need time and peace to cope with sorrow. In the Antarctic, there would be plenty of both. Somehow I carried on with my preparations. I continued with the daily round of meeting sponsors, dealt with the thousand and one details that remained, and persevered with my training, even if everything had now become a burden.

Much had been destroyed for many of those who had been close to Berit. I had been full of expectations, but now they had been swept away and replaced by emptiness. I fell prey to chaotic emotions; I felt as if I was doing things that were important in one way but at the same time wholly insignificant. I began to look forward to the day when I would be alone on the Antarctic ice.

YOU CAN ACHIEVE
WHAT YOU WANT

Not infrequently, when I was out in the mountains in a blizzard or storm, my thoughts would turn to the old pioneers. What must it have been like to be Roald Amundsen? I let my imagination run free to the point where I could almost feel that I was in his place.

Few people understand where on earth I got the "crazy idea" of skiing to the South Pole alone. Most focus exclusively on the physical and mental struggle associated with such demanding enterprises and lack the experience that would enable them to conceive what such an expedition would be like. It's interesting to consider what it is that really drives someone to realize an ambition, whether it concerns the South Pole or some other extraordinary goal. My dream of attaining the South Pole didn't arise exclusively from historical reading; it was also a need to try myself to the limit.

Research has been carried out into precisely what drives some people to seek the kind of thrills and challenges that are completely alien to most others. Professor Gunnar Breivik of the Norwegian School of Sport Sciences published a report on the subject, showing that the blood of those who practice dangerous sports has been found to contain extremely low levels of a certain enzyme that regulates the effect of stress on mental activity. Breivik believes that such people are particularly prone to seeking out situations that expose them to physical or mental strain. It is also his view that they experience stress as more positive and enjoyable than others with a normal level of the enzyme. Statistical analysis suggests that this desire for heightened sensory stimulation is largely hereditary, approximately 70 percent, with 30 percent due to environmental factors. About 10 percent of the population have this need. The form it takes is often decided by environment. It may be expressed in dangerous activities and occupations like mountain climbing and police work but may also find an outlet in joyriding, drug addiction, or crime.

Other researchers believe that those who seek a life of action also unconsciously acquire a more profound understanding of how they function mentally. It's not natural for human beings to keep still, even though until quite recently in our civilization it has been abnormal to move more than was absolutely necessary. In the past, much energy has been expended on physical work. Only during the last hundred years, as a result of industrialization and the advance of sedentary office work, have physical exercise and physical education been practiced for their own sake.

When we start playing, the world begins to open. Little by little we learn the difference between throwing a stone, which drops like a dead weight, and throwing a ball, which bounces. We travel more quickly between points A and B by cycling instead of walking. Through climbing, playing with a ball, jumping, and dancing, the brain learns how the body adapts to the surroundings. That's been my personal experience. My childhood with a lot of play and climbing in the big chestnut tree, all the winters with skis and sleds, and subsequent active participation in various sports have taught me how to coordinate my mental processes with physical reaction.

As a travel guide on Svalbard, I often observed how differently people react in rough terrain. Where some move freely and naturally, others have to crouch down and grip tightly to keep their balance. Compared with many continental Europeans, we Norwegians have a clear advantage in our background: playing and moving in rough and undulating terrain, particularly skiing, gives us a good sense of balance.

Imagination is necessary to put oneself in another's shoes or to attain a goal. Children have a powerful imagination. Presumably, I was inspired by thoughts of the South Pole and other polar adventures during a period when I was particularly receptive. My brother, Sigmund, who is two years younger, had the same upbringing I had and was also with me at Polhøgda, but he doesn't even remember the visit. I remember that he was engrossed with my father's excavator, which stood outside. Today, Sigmund is a builder.

As I child I was always told, "You can achieve what you want." I was also told that I had a strong will and was appallingly pigheaded. Only when I grew up did I understand how I could profit from these qualities. During the planning and preparation of my expedition to the South Pole, I was surprised at my own willpower.

The constant question both before and after such an enterprise is always *why?* Was it a craving for publicity, something to do with feminism, or an urge to prove how strong I was? Why go to the North or South Pole when this has been done before? Why on earth climb Everest when nearly 600 people already have? Why write poems when so many have already been written? Why compose music? Why do people work to the point of exhaustion in order to acquire status symbols and heart disease?

Every age has had its own particular form of expressing the creative urge and giving vent to vitality. Those of us who aren't artists must try to make something else out of life. What we do and why we do it have as many variations as there are human beings. What drove me was a combination of my upbringing, childhood surroundings, social influences, and way of life in adulthood, to which must be added my old dream of the South Pole, a taste for testing myself mentally and physically, an enjoyment of long tours, and, above all, a love for skiing.

A desire to go to the South Pole isn't an impulsive idea. It is a long, drawn-out process. You can't get the idea in May and set off in October. Success means living with the idea year after year until it matures.

FROM THE COLD NORTH
TO THE FREEZING SOUTH

Of course, I was far from being the first Norwegian attracted by these inhospitable regions. Through the years, many of my compatriots have been drawn to the Antarctic and remain so to this day. They believe somehow that the continent is a piece of their homeland. This is attributable above all to Roald Amundsen. On December 14, 1911, he reached the South Pole, the first to do so. What strikes a chord in most Norwegians is not so much that Amundsen planted his country's flag at the South Pole but that he won the longest and most famous ski race in history.

Norwegian and indeed all modern Antarctic exploration began in 1892, with the cruise of the *Jason,* commanded by the legendary whaling captain C. A. Larsen. In the Weddell Sea along the coast of Antarctica, he discovered what is now known as Oscar II Coast. He also became the first to find fossils, which took the form of petrified trees. That was the first evidence that about seventy million years ago Antarctica was warm, fertile, and full of animal life. Now it's the coldest, driest, and most icebound of the continents. It's also the most inaccessible, with the harshest climate on earth.

Antarctica is bigger than all of Western Europe; by comparison, it's forty times the area of Norway or the size of the United States and Mexico together. Ice covers 98 percent of its surface and is more than 4,000 meters (two and a half miles) thick at its highest point. The South Pole lies at an altitude of 2,850 meters (nearly 10,000 feet), most of it solid ice. If all the Antarctic ice melted, the oceans would rise by seventy meters (225 feet) and most of the great cities of the world would be drowned. East Antarctica would then consist of one large island and West Antarctica of several smaller ones. The huge mass of ice isn't static: it flows like some exceedingly viscous fluid, sometimes as much as two kilometers (a mile and a quarter) during the course of a year. One of the longest mountain ranges in the world, the Transantarctic Mountains, runs right across the continent. Its summit, and the highest point of Antarctica, is Mount Vinson, rising 4,892 meters (16,050 feet) above sea level.

Norway has an Antarctic possession, Queen Maud Land, annexed during the 1930s. It covers one-seventh of the Antarctic continent and is about seven times the area of Norway. The purpose of the annexation was to secure whaling rights in the adjacent waters, but national claims in general, and Norwegian claims in particular, have never been universally recognized in Antarctica.

Until 1960, Norway had a significant presence in the Antarctic. At that time, we still had a considerable whale fishery in the Southern Ocean, with permanently manned bases on South Georgia. From the end of the 1970s until 1993, the Norwegian Polar Institute organized five scientific expeditions, and in the southern summer of 1989–90 a permanent Norwegian base, Troll, was established in the Gjelsvik Mountains in Queen Maud Land. However, an official Norwegian presence in the Antarctic has always been somewhat limited. Private expeditions have done most of the work. Between the world wars, for example, Lars Christensen, who owned one of the big Norwegian whaling companies, personally financed various expeditions that, among other things, discovered Queen Maud Land.

Nonetheless, it always comes back to Roald Amundsen. In

most ways, his journey to the South Pole in 1910–12 has been the model for subsequent Norwegian expeditions. In the first place, this is due to his use of skis and dogs. At a deeper level, his meticulous planning, his lack of masochism and heroic posturing, and, above all, his realization that an enterprise that's not enjoyable isn't worth doing have led the way.

The Norwegian South Polar Expedition of 1990–91 was the first in the spirit of Amundsen. This was also, in fact, the first Norwegian expedition to attain the South Pole after he did. Like Amundsen, the Norwegian South Polar Expedition used dogs, which are now prohibited in Antarctica, and also had several depots along the way. Unlike Amundsen, the later expedition started not from the Ross Sea but from the Weddell Sea, in West Antarctica. Sjur Mørdre, one of the participants who was in charge of logistics, pioneered the route from Berkner Island, which was followed by Erling Kagge in 1992–93, when he became the first ever to reach the South Pole alone and unsupported.

This was the route followed in 1994 by the Norwegian Unarmed Expedition of Cato Zahl-Pedersen, Odd Harald Hauge, and Lars Ebbesen. It took its name from the fact that Zahl-Pedersen had lost his arms in an accident. They set off at the same time as I did. I chose a different route, from Hercules Inlet on the Ronne Ice Shelf. This way I would be completely on my own. Had I started from the same place as the other expedition, it would have been a completely different journey, with an element of competition that didn't interested me one bit. I had no plans for a race to the South Pole; it was pure chance that we happened to travel at the same time. In any case, the flight to Berkner Island from the base at Patriot Hills would have cost another $72,500 that I didn't have.

No one had yet taken precisely the route that I had chosen. It followed the meridian of 80°30′ west. The distance to the Pole was 1,200 kilometers (750 miles). Some years earlier, Reinhold

Messner had followed a similar route, but he was flown to 82° south and traveled via the Thiel Mountains, where he had arranged for a supply of food and fuel. I proposed to give these mountains a wide berth, keeping them well to the east. My route was 200 kilometers (125 miles) shorter than that from Berkner Island. Someone alleged in a newspaper article that I had started in the wrong place and that my route was too short. It's a matter of definition. Today, one can be flown anywhere, such that in a sense any overland expedition is artificial. Before the age of air travel, Antarctic explorers had to use ships, and by necessity their snow journeys began where open water ended. All things considered, now it's reasonable to start at the edge of the continent. This ensures climbing the whole way up to the icecap, which was the essence of the old pioneering expeditions. My starting point at Hercules Inlet lies where continental land meets the sea, even though the latter is perennially covered by shelf ice. Berkner Island lies farther out on the Ronne Ice Shelf. Starting there involves traveling 500 kilometers (312 miles) at sea level before beginning the climb up to the polar plateau.

That I had planned an expedition that was "too short" was the last thing on my mind when I finally settled back in my aircraft seat on October 24, 1994, on my way to Chile. I thought that the 1,200 kilometers (750 miles) I proposed covering in fifty days were long enough. Besides, I was the first to try my particular route to the South Pole, which was enough to cause me some trepidation.

It was a relief at last to put Oslo and all the preparations behind me. My sleds had been sent ahead two weeks earlier to ensure that they arrived in time. They contained everything necessary for my expedition.

Even though planning had begun in good time, a hundred and one details had to be dealt with at the last minute. The most depressing aspect of going on a low-budget expedition alone is that you have to do everything yourself. In the end, I just shrugged it off when something or someone obstructed me. "Be as discouraging and difficult as you like," I thought. "I'll manage anyway."

Modern polar travelers don't need to winter in the snows in order to be able to start at the right time, which is at the beginning of the summer. Things are complicated in the Antarctic, because the southern summer is winter in our hemisphere. We simply buy airline tickets and save an entire year that way compared to the pioneers, who had to go south by sea, usually in boats that were slow even by the standards of the day. You have to be fairly blasé if you're unimpressed by the fact that today we can travel to virtually the farthest north and south points on the surface of the globe in twenty hours or so. In comparison with the expeditions of the old heroes, this helps even more to put my own journey in perspective.

STEAK AND RED WINE IN CHILE—AND WE'RE OFF

Julie Maske, with whom I had crossed Greenland, joined me in Santiago de Chile. She was to help with the final packing and also accompany me to ANI's base at Patriot Hills to do some video recording and take stills before I started. Together, we flew on to Punta Arenas, in the Straits of Magellan, the southernmost town in Chile. Julie speaks Spanish, which turned out to be invaluable. My sleds had been sent on by a big international forwarding agent, with a guaranteed delivery date, but now they were stuck in Santiago.

It was All Saints' Day, which, at these latitudes, meant that thousands of flowers were considered more important than some heavy packages from Norway. Both the other Norwegian expedition and I were utterly dependent on catching the flight to Patriot Hills with all our baggage as planned, and we suffered some nerve-racking days together. The Norwegian embassy in Santiago and the consulate in Punta Arenas worked overtime to help, and at midnight the day before departure we were able to go out to the airfield to get our packages. We drove right onto the runway, entered a fuselage, and pointed out our items of cargo. A customs official had been persuaded to get up in the middle of the night, and an hour later, the Norwegian vice consul had piled everything into a friend's garage. The final check of food and equipment could begin.

In Punta Arenas we were staying at the Hotel Condor Plata, named after the silver condor, which is what the Indigenous tribes in the region called the first aircraft they saw. Previous expeditions had also stayed at the hotel, and the walls were covered with pictures and autographs. Immediately outside the door of our room was a large photograph of a wrecked airplane with the caption "The End of an Adventure." It pictured a German flying pioneer who had been killed when he crashed into a lake a little north of Punta Arenas.

To avoid sharing the same fate, we went over to the statue of the Indigenous guide who followed Magellan, the Portuguese navigator after whom the strait was named, while he was exploring Patagonia. It's the custom of all travelers in the region to kiss the toes of this statue in order to secure a safe return. We kissed the worn and polished toe and took photographs. Then we went out on the town, had a steak, drank some good red wine, smoked a cigar, and said farewell to city life. The following day we sat in the Hercules aircraft that was to fly us over the sea to the base at Patriot Hills.

ANI has been engaged in commercial flying here since 1985 and is alone in providing private flying service in these parts. Consequently, it is without competition, which is reflected in its prices. The company was run at that time by Anne Kershaw, whose husband, Giles Kershaw, was one of the modern Antarctic flying pioneers. He discovered places where it was possible to land, and he was one of the founders of ANI. He was killed in a crash in 1990 on the Antarctic Peninsula while flying an autogiro.

It's hard to fly commercially in Antarctica. The season is short and utterly dependent on the weather. The site at Patriot Hills was chosen because of its blue ice, a hard surface that makes a serviceable runway. The Hercules aircraft used by ANI is chartered from South African Air and flown by bush pilots, who usually transport food and equipment for aid projects in Africa.

They are really tough characters. What we didn't know beforehand was that they had never landed on ice before. It was just as well, because we had heard more than enough stories of bumpy landings at Patriot Hills, and I had visions of the expedition ending there. We had seven hours to imagine the worst.

It's not at all enjoyable to fly in a Hercules. You don't notice when you take off, and you feel shut in and completely isolated in flight. Admittedly, comfortable seats had been installed in our aircraft, and there were two apertures, glazed with frosted glass, through which we could observe the surroundings. What's more, we had an "air hostess" in the person of Holly, the general gofer at the ANI office in Punta Arenas. She served sandwiches and Coca-Cola during the flight. The noise was deafening, and it was hard to keep up a conversation. The earplugs we were given before starting kept out most of the noise, and I slept for most of the flight.

Besides Julie and the Norwegian Unarmed Expedition, together with its photographer, Knut Bry, we also had an NRK (Norwegian Broadcasting Corporation) correspondent in South America to do some color stories before our respective starts. Also on the flight were a film crew on the way to the emperor penguin colony north of Berkner Island and a Japanese expedition aiming for the South Pole as well.

The leader of the Japanese expedition, Susumu Nakumura, was something of a veteran. He had been to the North Pole and had climbed Mount Everest, and now he was going "solo" to the South Pole. That is to say, he had three snowmobiles with him to make a path and transport food and equipment. He would be running on light cross-country skis with light cross-country bindings.

We landed on November 2 at 6:00 a.m. The landing went well—a little shaky, but in the huge aircraft we didn't notice much. The passengers were noticeably relieved at being safely down. The sun was high in the heavens and—a rarity in these parts—it was dead calm. Even with the thermometer showing –20 degrees Celsius (–4 degrees Fahrenheit), it didn't feel cold, undoubtedly because the air was so dry.

The base at Patriot Hills was a camp—a large mess tent, a communications tent, and a large number of small tents for tourists. Those of us going on long journeys lived in our own tents. To stay in the camp cost a thousand Norwegian kroner (£100 or $145) per day. Visitors would often remain at Patriot Hills for a few days before being flown or transported by snowmobile to their destinations.

The base manager was a calm, pleasant Briton named Geoff Somers, who was on Will Steger's seven-month Transantarctic Expedition of 1989–90. They started near the tip of the Antarctic Peninsula, traveled with dog teams via numerous depots to the South Pole, and then went on to the coast on the other side, around 90° east, via the Russian research stations.

Betty Menard, from Alaska, was the radio operator at Patriot Hills, and I arranged times and procedures with her for my weekly radio contacts. The station maintained radio contact with the head office in Punta Arenas and, when necessary, with the Amundsen-Scott Base at the South Pole. Betty kept in constant contact with the head office and with all aircraft and fixed camps belonging to ANI in the area. She had a busy job. For a few hours every day, the satellite telephone was switched on so that we could ring home.

Nina, one of the two cooks at the base, was Anglo-Norwegian. Highly adventurous, she had chosen an occupation that enabled her to move around, and the combination of guide and cook had taken her to many different places. Nina and the other cook, Tanya, produced the most incredible dishes. There were no freeze-dried rations here but instead fresh vegetables and other supplies flown in weekly from Punta Arenas.

From Patriot Hills, ANI organizes climbs on Mount Vinson, arranges visits to the emperor penguin colony near Berkner Island, and generally provides support for expeditions. Visitors fall into two categories. One consists of rather special tourists who have two things in common: a taste for adventure and a great deal of money. The other consists of polar travelers like myself. We also have two things in common: a taste for adventure and very little money.

All the expeditions spent the time at Patriot Hills on final preparations and one last overhaul of their equipment. The Japanese were busy working out how much gasoline they really needed. They had miscalculated at home and brought too little. Petrol cost about £8 per liter (about $42 a gallon) at Patriot Hills, so their calculators were clicking away, and there was frequent contact with the moneybags in Tokyo.

The Unarmed Expedition members were also quite occupied—with photography. Photographer Knut Bry was bubbling over with crazy angles and ideas. I watched Cato Zahl-Petersen hauling a sled. He had lost one entire arm and the other below the elbow while climbing a high-tension electric pylon when he was young. Since then he has been a pioneer in showing what people with a disability can achieve. Knowing as I do how one struggles to haul a heavy sled even with two whole arms, and particularly how one depends on them in such circumstances, it was incredible that he dared to set off on such a journey. Even though he did all his own hauling, he clearly needed much help in other things. For that reason, the tour was also an achievement on the part of his companions, Lars Ebbesen and Odd Harald Hauge. Cato's disability was plainly visible, but some might say that all of us who start on a journey of this nature have some disability, which often might be less easy to detect.

When I saw those three men pack themselves into their little tent, I felt like a princess in mine. I wasn't at all sorry to be traveling alone. It was simple to be on my own. I would have to depend on myself, and I could blame nobody else if anything went wrong, if something had been forgotten, or if something didn't function. I had repeatedly gone through the sled with my checklist and did so now one last time. I was sleeping in my own tent, everything was in order, and I was ready to start.

We took photograph after photograph and many videos. Poor Julie—I wasn't very patient, and in the photographs I looked fretful. I was thinking only of getting underway.

On the afternoon of November 4, Aaron and Mark from ANI drove me down to the ice shelf by snowmobile. The trip to Hercules Inlet took five hours, and I was taken eighty kilometers (fifty miles) in the "wrong" direction. Naturally, I could have set off from Patriot Hills, but the point was to start down on the ice shelf.

On the way, we passed *Ice Princess,* an aircraft that had crashed the year before while landing in a whiteout. The big DC-6 will remain there forever. At present it's quite visible, but eventually it will be covered in ice and snow. To be rescued from the Antarctic is expensive, whether for an aircraft or for a human being. I took the wreck as a reminder to be careful, especially in a whiteout. Aaron and Mark invited me to their tent for a farewell dinner of noodles and white wine. Around midnight, I staggered over to my own tent.

We got up early the next day, to test the radio among other things. We programmed the frequencies, which, since I had left the instructions at home in Oslo, took nearly an hour. We couldn't make contact with Patriot Hills, presumably because Betty was no longer on watch, but crackling indicated that we had done something correctly, at least so we thought.

Aaron started his snowmobile around eleven o'clock. They had Julie's camera and drove around a few times to take pictures of the start before heading back to Patriot Hills.

I stood for a moment watching them and then began to move.

ALONE AT LAST

At last, the day I had been looking forward to, consciously or unconsciously, for nearly thirty years had arrived. It had been a long and tortuous path; now there were few ways back and only one direction to my goal, 1,200 kilometers (750 miles) straight ahead.

However, any feelings of happiness and expectation were completely absent. I felt utterly tired, and that was all. The murder of Berit, the struggle to find sponsors, and the farewells at home all overwhelmed me once I found myself alone. All I wanted to do was pitch my tent, creep into my sleeping bag, and go to sleep. But the sun was shining from a cloudless sky, and my typically Norwegian upbringing got the upper hand. We have pangs of conscience if we stay indoors in good weather, so I started the climb up toward Fusco Nunatak.

I had decided in advance to take it easy the first week in order to accustom my body to the effort and the cold. Nonetheless, during the first two or three days, I drove myself hard up the hummocks to get rid of my gloomy thoughts. It was steep, but not too steep to climb with skis and sled. With a load of a hundred kilos (220 pounds), of which fifteen kilos were in my rucksack, it was slow business going upward. Nonetheless, it felt good to be on skis once more and using my powers.

Gradually, I began to feel keyed up and tingled with excitement at the thought of the kilometers that lay before me. The wind was dead against me, the temperature −20 degrees Celsius

And so it begins. Photograph by Julie Maske.

(−4 degrees Fahrenheit). I felt no great sense of isolation, which was hardly surprising, since it was only eighty kilometers (fifty miles) back to Patriot Hills. Should difficulties arise at an early stage, I would need only return to the base. For about a week, I could reach it in a day or two, even allowing for the fact that my course was well to the east of the route we came down on the snowmobile.

The weather was fine, with good visibility, and the terrain rose in a succession of terraces. I passed some narrow crevasses now and then. In the distance, I could see blue ice and huge open chasms, luckily to the east of my course.

I was prepared to dump some of the load in the sled and relay up the steepest hummocks, but as it turned out I was able to move everything in one go by traversing the steepest slopes diagonally or by simply going around. Now and then there was a true struggle between the sled and me; it tried to drag me down, but I wanted to go up. My skis slid backward, and once or twice I had to kneel down and haul for dear life on the ski poles, but I won our little struggle each time. The surface was rock-hard, wind-packed drift snow, but all things considered, the skins under my skis gripped well.

After ten kilometers, with a vertical climb of 420 meters (1,365 feet), I was satisfied with the day's work and made camp. It was impossible to find a level tent site, so I had to make do with a night on a slope. It wasn't easy to pitch the tent on the hard surface, and I bent a few pegs before I grasped that I had to drill holes with ice screws. I melted snow and made dinner. As it was important to establish a routine, I took out the cake my mother had baked in order to cut a piece for dessert. I would do this each Saturday of my expedition.

I had a sharp new sheath knife—a copy of the one Roald Amundsen had taken to the South Pole. Just as I was thinking that I must take care not to cut myself, the knife slipped and made a fairly deep cut in my finger. Already, on the first day in Antarctica, the first-aid kit was needed, and I pulled the wound together with an adhesive bandage. It had been a trying day with many a heavy heave, and I fell asleep on my way into my sleeping bag. That first night, I slept deeply for twelve solid hours.

The next day it was snowing, with poor visibility. It was blowing hard, with driving snow, and I set my course by following the sastrugi rather than the compass. After a few hours, my ski poles hit solid blue ice. The vision of the crevassed field of blue ice that I had seen the previous day flashed through my head, and I felt my heart begin to pound faster. In the driving snow, I had strayed too far to the left and cursed myself for having been so slovenly with the compass. There was no point in taking risks among crevasses in zero visibility, so I turned and went back a hundred meters to pitch my tent. I examined the tent site carefully, probing with skis and ski poles to test the consistency underfoot. If either skis or poles could be driven deep, there was probably a hidden crevasse below. Where I made camp, it was hard and firm.

My GPS revealed that I had covered twelve more kilometers and gained 410 meters (1,344 feet) of altitude. It also confirmed that I had strayed quite far to the east. According to the map, I was in an area with large crevasses. I was in the middle of what had seemed so frightening from the ice shelf down below. Should I turn and go down again?

The next morning there was a total whiteout, so I turned over in my sleeping bag and slept on. Around ten o'clock it cleared up to reveal crevassed blue ice as far as the eye could see both to the east and to the west. The area with the open crevasses that I had observed at the start was nowhere to be seen. Probably it was even further east. I was under the ridge where the crevasses seemed like zebra stripes against the blue ice. I remembered what I had promised Einar before I left home: faced with crevasses, I was to circumvent them. On the other hand, I had little desire to lose any of the altitude I'd gained with so much toil.

From my previous experience of glaciers, I knew that snow bridges were often strong enough to be safely crossed on skis. Here the crevasses seemed to be filled with hard, wind-packed drift snow, so it seemed safe enough even under a load of food and fuel. I chose to carry on straight ahead rather than risk blundering into what seemed even more dangerous terrain. I attached my compass mounting to my belt and decided to hold my course as best I could. I laid my skis on the sled, put on my crampons, and, with the help of my ski poles, climbed straight up.

The first ten or fifteen crevasses were no more than one to three meters across. Where blue ice and drift snow met, there was coarse-grained snow that tumbled down into the depths when I probed its edges with my ski poles. I broke through knee-deep at one point and then put on my skis. The gap between ice and snow bridge might be anything up to fifty centimeters (twenty inches), and I could see far down into the crevasse with its characteristic delicate blue tints. It was beautiful but also frightening, and I shuddered at the sight. The glacier was so steep that I had to put on my crampons on the blue ice between each crevasse. Even though my skis had steel edges and skins, they slithered all over the ice.

I spent nearly a whole day this way, alternating between crampons and skis. My body temperature alternated too. I was ice-cold while making the changes but then sweated while hauling the sled straight up. At the widest crevasses, I was a bit worried about air pockets, so I crossed over in my best Pink Panther style: long, delicate steps, so my weight was evenly distributed over both of my 210-centimeter-long (seven-foot) skis. The sled, with its similar length, also distributed its weight splendidly.

I was never really afraid, just intensely focused. It was a situation for which I had mentally prepared myself—I had imagined falling into a crevasse and gone over in my mind how I'd cope with the situation. I often thought of Douglas Mawson, the Australian explorer. If I were to fall into a crevasse I would follow his example.

In March 1912, when Amundsen reached Hobart, in Tasmania, on *Fram*, he gave Mawson some of his dogs. Mawson was about to begin a fateful enterprise, and the story of his journey back to base after he had lost two companions is one of the most dramatic episodes in polar history. At this point in my own journey, it was constantly at the back of my mind.

Mawson, a geologist by profession, had been on Shackleton's expedition of 1907–9, during which he accomplished a sled journey of 1,200 kilometers (750 miles), without dogs, to the South Magnetic Pole in South Victoria Land.

Now he was leading his own Antarctic expedition, which had largely scientific aims. The goal was to explore the coast between Adélie Land and Queen Mary Land, and in December 1912, two parties landed at different points. This was the first occasion on which radio was used in the Antarctic, with contact between the bases on land and *Aurora*, the expedition ship. Mawson had planned for several extensive sled trips into the interior but had no intention of reaching the South Pole. On the other hand, he reached the South Magnetic Pole again, this time from the west Antarctic coast.

The first accident occurred on the Commonwealth Glacier, when Mawson drove his dog team over a crevasse that he thought was safe. When he turned around, he couldn't see one of his companions, Lt. Belgrave Ninnis, or his dog team. Mawson and his other companion, Dr. Xavier Mertz, a Swiss mountaineer, who had gone ahead on skis to find a path, went back and found a bottomless hole. All they could see and hear were two injured dogs stuck on a ledge a little way down. The sled swallowed by the crevasse contained vital food and equipment. Everything was lost, and the journey back for the two survivors became a nightmare. They had hardly any food for themselves and none for the dogs. They had to eat the last six dogs to survive. Mertz fell ill with a high fever and died, probably of an overdose of vitamin A from eating too much dog liver. For three weeks, hungry and freezing, Mawson struggled back toward his base over sinister terrain.

One day, he broke through a snow bridge and remained dangling on the rope with which he was hauling his sled. Beneath him was the abyss. Now on the verge of exhaustion, he was tempted to cut the rope and end it all. However, he summoned up all his remaining strength and, with aid of loops, managed to drag himself up the four meters of rope. When he emerged from the crevasse and seized hold of the sled, it sank deeper, and once more he found himself suspended over the depths. With almost superhuman willpower he managed to climb up the rope once more and finally saved himself from the crevasse.

Later on, starving, frozen, and exhausted, Mawson was on the verge of giving up when he stumbled on a cairn erected by a relief party. In the cairn was a cache of food, together with a note of the position and a message that *Aurora* had returned and was waiting for Mawson and his men. The irony of the situation was that the relief party had left the cairn that same morning at eight o'clock and Mawson arrived at two o'clock that afternoon. He spent two days eating, resting, and recuperating before continuing on his way. After being weather-bound in a snow cave for a week, he finally reached the coast, just in time to see the ship depart. Arriving at the base, he met five men who had agreed to wait and search for him and his party. *Aurora* was recalled by radio but was unable to force a passage through the quickly forming ice. Mawson and his companions were forced to remain behind for another winter.

I too had loops in the rope with which I was hauling my sled. In addition, I had two ice screws fitted with loops of rope, which theoretically I could use to climb out of a crevasse. I also had an easily accessible emergency tracking radio transmitter in the top of my rucksack. But I knew very well that if I did fall into a crevasse, I might easily be injured or trapped by snow and ice. If I couldn't climb out unaided, it wouldn't be long before I froze to death. Unless ANI fortuitously had an aircraft directly overhead, the weather was good, and it was possible to land, the emergency transmitter wouldn't be of much practical help. There was every reason to be careful when negotiating crevasses. Where I found big air pockets close to the blue ice, I found another crossing.

On the third day I was still in the crevassed area for five or six hours. It was slow business picking my way ahead. Nonetheless, I had moved another ten kilometers to the south and 200 meters (650 feet) vertically upward. When I made camp, I could see the undulating plateau that led to the South Pole.

By and large, I was satisfied with the day's work and hoped that I had finished with crevasses for a while. As I lay in my sleeping bag, I could feel my right elbow throbbing after all the ramming with a ski pole to test the snow bridges.

It was splendid traveling alone. My reason for going solo to the South Pole had never been because I wanted to be the first woman to do so, even though it helped me to raise the necessary funds. I was alone because I didn't know anyone with the same overwhelming desire to go to the South Pole. It seemed somehow wrong if others had to be persuaded to come on a tour like this.

I like traveling with others, but I've been on trips where my companions have mentally collapsed and almost had to be poured out of their sleeping bags before we could go on. It's an unpleasant experience to enjoy yourself while simultaneously being aware that the person next to you is utterly miserable. It's difficult to admit to yourself that you're not in control of the situation and even more difficult to admit it to your companions.

I remembered all those who, before my departure, thought that being on my own would be the worst part of an expedition such as mine. On the contrary, even though I'm no lone wolf, it was being alone for so long that I most looked forward to. Solitude is just as necessary as food and sleep; only in that way can you find calm and make contact with yourself. Workaday life is often so hectic that it's hard to think a single thought right through. I looked forward to finding an inner peace, to remember, to philosophize, and to think ahead.

Admittedly, before this ski tour, I had never sampled complete isolation except for a week in a mountain cabin to cram for an exam. In purely practical terms, everything is easier and quicker when you're alone. There's no one else to consider. You can make the day's stage as long—or short—as you like, follow a routine that suits you, and make camp when you're tired. After two years in Antarctica, the modern Norwegian explorer Johan Gjæver once wrote, "Two men are ideal, three is one too many, ten men is hell." I thought that one woman was absolutely perfect.

WIND, WEATHER, AND PROPER CLOTHING

After a few days, I had settled down to a good rhythm, with other things than crevasses to worry about. The sun was shining, but a wind was blowing obliquely from the west. To cope with this, I worked out a particular traveling technique: I simply leaned against the wind. Until I found the right headgear, I had a headache the first few days because of the noise and the draft. Despite the cold, I dripped with sweat when I wore my windproof cap; with my woolen one alone, it was too drafty. Eventually, I learned how to dress according to the temperature and wind velocity.

Wind and weather could vary from hour to hour. It could change from a heavy gale to a light breeze, from blazing sunshine to whiteout, all in the course of a single day. Snow conditions were just as temperamental. There were the everlasting sastrugi and the horrible drift snow as sticky as glue, not to mention the wind-packed crust with a surface as hard as rock. On the crust, at least, the sled seemed light as a feather. Unfortunately, throughout the whole tour, drift snow predominated.

The most gruesome thing I knew as a child was when we visited Mølen, near Nevlunghavn on the Norwegian coast, during a storm, and I saw the huge waves hurling themselves against the shore. I have no idea whether it was experiences like these that made me frightened of the sea, but I've always felt safest on land. I become seasick at the merest ripple.

In the mountains, however, I've always felt at home. For as long as I can remember, my family has always spent the winter and Easter holidays on skis, either up in the mountains or closer to home in Krokskogen, near Oslo. There was never any fuss or bother on these trips. Enjoying ourselves was vital, and up in the mountains, the view and a good downhill run were more important than the number of miles covered. When the weather was bad, I would carry on skiing after the rest of the family had finished. I have never understood why people choose to stay indoors when they can be outside.

At an early age I learned how to dress for all kinds of weather, and as an orienteer I knew to always have a compass in my anorak pocket. Nonetheless, I have known what it is like to lose my bearings in bad weather with inadequate clothing and poor equipment. I discovered that even though I was suitably chastened, fear didn't have the upper hand. I was fascinated by the sensation of not being fully in control, of being on a knife-edge. I felt this to a greater degree when I began climbing and traveling on glaciers. I did orienteering on the same principle, never fully in control. I chose daring routes that would pay dividends if they worked but that involved risks if I didn't manage to keep my course. Something within me rebelled at the thought of the safest choice. Very often my legs worked faster than my head, and I went around in circles. As a result, I was never a particularly brilliant orienteer, but it was exciting, and I enjoyed myself enormously.

Apart from crevasses, I had concluded in advance that low temperatures combined with wind and exhaustion would likely be the greatest peril. I have faced gales and blizzards in the Norwegian mountains, and on a range called Tafjordfjellene I was once in dire trouble. At a certain point, we were overtaken by a frightful storm at a temperature of −20 degrees Celsius (−4 degrees Fahrenheit). After a very short while, I grasped that I wasn't properly dressed. My anorak was too thin, and my body was racked with cold. Finally, we reached a point where we could no longer move because of the wind. It was impossible to pitch our tents, but after a little while we found a hummock, in which we began digging a snow cave. Since we only had two shovels, we had to take turns. During a rest, I sat down. I became cold and sluggish, and after a little while, the cold felt good; in fact, I felt warm. Luckily, my companions noticed what was happening. I was shaken and roused and put to digging until first the sensation of cold returned and then warmth.

Some years later, I was in the Jotunheimen Mountains together with another party. No one wanted to be the first to say that enough was enough. We had wanted to reach the Olvasbu cabin but finally had to give up. It was cold and dark, with fiercely driving snow. We stopped and made camp, and some of my companions were so frozen that they had difficulty pitching their tents and lighting their Primus stoves. I discovered how big, strong, hulking men became exhausted, frightened, and petulant. Finally, we managed to creep into our tents, but not before many of us had learned a lesson or two about skiing companions and the choice of equipment. None of us went ski touring together again.

The strongest wind I've ever experienced was when I was lifted bodily by a squall of hurricane. It was after that experience, incidentally, that I really discovered that Norwegians are world champions in outdoor life. When my fellow countrymen heard of this particular episode, many explained that they'd felt exactly the same kind of wind and had had difficulty pitching a tent. It's basically impossible to pitch a tent in storm-force winds. Usually, people are only faced with a light gale before putting up a tent or retreating into a mountain cabin.

All in all, one has to be well prepared for a ski tour! The only thing I really missed in the Antarctic was a bivouac sack, in which

All my equipment worked perfectly.

I could take refuge during my hourly breaks to rest and eat. On the other hand, the fact that I had to make so few repairs along the way is proof that in general I had taken the right equipment.

Before arriving at the South Pole, I had traveled for nearly 500 hours on my skis. They are of the Telemark type, with steel edges and wax-free bases, and incredibly tough. Many times I've run straight into hard sastrugi and once or twice feared that my skis would snap. Against that event, I carried polyester fabric and epoxy resin glue to make repairs.

My ski boots were fantastic. I didn't have a single blister, and they kept my feet warm and dry during the whole journey. Next to my skin, I wore thin woolen socks, then vapor-barrier socks, followed by thick Lapp felted woolen socks for insulation, and outermost another anti-condensation sock to prevent wear and tear on the felted woolen sock caused by the boot. My boots were of the ordinary Telemark style from Alfa, admittedly with uppers of cordura (nylon) instead of leather.

I used Super Telemark Rottefella toe bindings. I also took

along Kandahar cables, in case the toe attachment broke and I had to fix my boot by tension around the heel. The advantage of a toe binding is, of course, that it allows maximum freedom to lift the heel and therefore saves precious energy. Fortunately, I never needed the cables.

I found that skiing in Antarctica was rather odd. With a sled weighing a hundred kilos, mohair skins under my skis, and abrasive snow, there was no sliding. I had read that it rarely snowed in the Antarctic, but it did so properly and well the second day out and again at the halfway point. It was like skiing on sand. I say grandly that I skied to the South Pole. A better description would be that I stamped and trudged there.

What I had least of was clothing. Apart from my down jacket, which I wore while making and breaking camp, I had only the clothes I stood up in, besides a fleece jacket and trousers. Next to my skin I wore woolen underclothing, including a vest that had a high neck and zipper. During the first few weeks I only needed one layer under my microfiber anorak and trousers. The rest of the time I wore two layers of underclothing. My anorak and pants were reinforced at the knees and elbows. The double layer served as pockets, which, after four days, I filled with insulating material. During the whole journey, I skied with knee warmers made of angora. I kept beautifully warm as long as I was moving. In fact, I sweated when the sastrugi were high or the snow ridges steep.

Since it was the middle of the southern summer, the sun shone round the clock at those latitudes, so the tent was warmed during the night. As long as it wasn't overcast, the temperature in my tent could rise as high as 10–12 degrees Celsius (50–54 degrees Fahrenheit), and my clothes were beautifully dried by the morning. On previous ski tours, I had often lain shivering all night. When the next day dawned, and I had to continue on my way, I was quite worn out. Now, in the Antarctic, I slept like a log the whole night through and woke feeling quite rested. I only lay shivering on three or four occasions, when it was overcast and the wind shook the tent, making an awful noise.

I had an extreme cold weather sleeping bag, which had been fitted with a zipper. I had heard that the tent could be hot, but I didn't believe that on some nights I would end up sleeping with an open sleeping bag. During the first week on the polar plateau, with brilliant sunshine twenty-four hours a day, it was so warm on the side facing the sun that I went to sleep on the shady side. During the night, the sun had naturally circled round the horizon, so that each morning I woke on the sunny side, lovely and warm, and it was sheer pleasure crawling out of my sleeping bag.

I had two sleeping mats, whose surfaces were grooved. The function of the grooves was to collect the condensation from the sleeping bag. As soon as I took the mats out into the cold, the moisture froze, and all I needed to do was to shake off the ice that had formed.

My tent was of the same type used by the Norwegian explorer Børge Ousland on his solo journey to the North Pole in March–April 1994. The outer tent was made of ripstop nylon and was incredibly tough. If it gets torn, the damage stops right there and the fabric doesn't unravel any further. My tent was slightly torn at the beginning, presumably by some sharp piece of ice sailing through the wind. I mended it with spinnaker tape, and it held for the rest of the journey.

The inner tent was made of superlight nylon. It was in the shape of a tunnel, with three hoops. The poles were taped together at the joints, so they lay ready assembled in the channels. Furthermore, the hoops were also attached to the cups on one side of the tent. Since the hoops lay ready in the channels, all that remained was to insert them in the cups on the other side. The tent lay uppermost on the sled, with the ends of the hoops sticking out at the rear. When I wanted to pitch the tent, I first of all secured it to myself with a carabiner to prevent it from

Morning in a blizzard. I'm ready to dig out my sled.

blowing away. Next, I drove in the pegs at the back, which always faced into the wind. The door was on the lee side. I could make camp with mittens on, and it took only a few minutes. Occasionally, the snow was so hard that it was difficult to drive in the tent pegs. Then I needed to use ice screws, both as drills and as pegs.

When the wind was particularly strong, I pulled the sled over the foot of the tent, to prevent the tent from flapping violently while I put in the pegs, secured the guys, and piled snow on the snow flaps. During the night, the sled lay crosswise of the wind, behind the tent, secured with snow anchors to stop it from being blown away.

My sled was also a copy of the one used by Børge Ousland on his North Pole expedition. It was raised high in front to make it slide more easily over sastrugi. In addition, the cover was exceptionally large, so that it could be used as a bivouac in case my tent was lost or destroyed. The greatest danger to the tent, the one I feared most, was the stove flaring up.

I hauled the sled with a long rope instead of shafts. In the first place, this automatically enabled the sled to find the path of least resistance between sastrugi. Also, I could go back to the sled during my rests without unharnessing.

My biggest surprise was the size of the sastrugi. At Patriot Hills, there were none, and it was a simple matter to haul the sled with unaided, wax-free skis. But out on the trail, the sastrugi were a meter high and more. To haul the sled in that kind of terrain and clear each succeeding crest, I had to use skins almost the whole way.

Until I had climbed up to the plateau, I had fifteen kilos (thirty-three pounds) in my rucksack in order to have more weight when I strained at the harness. For the rest of the journey, I only carried my emergency transmitter, tent pegs, and down jacket in the rucksack. In my pockets, I kept chocolate and biscuits. Thermoses lay at the front of the sled.

My ski poles were shorter than usual. On a tour like mine, there was little heaving on them, so I had no need for long ones. With short poles, you have the advantage of relaxing the shoulders better. Mine were of the light, strong, racing kind, with relatively small baskets. Since the snow was generally packed hard, these worked well.

I used an American stove of the Primus type, the burner a unit on its own, fitted into a windshield and connected by a length of pressure tubing to a separate, interchangeable fuel bottle to which the pump was fitted. I took four of these bottles, which allowed me to empty a whole gallon can of fuel at a time. That avoided the risk of a large, half-empty container. My fuel was Coleman white gas—highly refined unleaded gasoline. I lit the stove in the tent entrance, taking great care in doing so. White gas is horribly flammable; a little flash, and there's a hole in the tent cloth, which itself is highly flammable too. When the burner was roaring properly, I took it into the tent and put it on a small piece of thin plywood for stability and to prevent damage to the groundsheet. I would also take a little extra fuel, in case I was so cold that I needed to warm up the tent. My daily fuel consumption was about 250 milliliters (about half a pint).

My saucepan was manufactured by the research laboratory of the Norwegian Defense Forces. It was a development of the well-known Nansen cooker, with double walls, so constructed that all heat from the stove is forced into the gap and around the inner saucepan for maximum absorption.

As a sensible precaution, I had duplicate burners, GPS, and compasses. Furthermore, the tubes in the closing mechanism of the sled cover could be converted into spare ski poles. I also took spare screws, spinnaker tape and sewing thread to repair the tent and clothes, darning materials, and batteries.

I also took a small but comprehensive first-aid kit. As it turned out, the only pill I took was a painkiller, for a dreadful headache caused by the wind one day soon after starting. During the latter part of the journey, I had to use eye ointment every night. This was a consequence of having to arrange more ventilation in my facemask to prevent condensation and icing up. As a result, my eyes became rather sore from the draft. To give them a rest, I bound a kerchief around my head every night. With light round the clock, it was an indescribable relief to have a little darkness. Each morning, before starting out, I applied anti-cold lotion with a high sunblock factor to my face and lips.

At the start, I was struggling upward so much that sweat and condensation collected behind my facemask to the point where I decided to take it off. After a glance in the mirror in the evening, I realized that, come what may, the mask had to stay on. One day without it had resulted in a couple of cold sores on my face. Later, I had a few minor sores even with the mask. It was particularly cold around the jaw; a beard would definitely have been a blessing.

Answering the calls of nature in deep cold is always a bit of a problem. I took with me a urine bottle made especially for women, which supposedly could be put into one's trousers, but that didn't work. In the morning, my "bathroom" was a hole that I dug in the tent entrance. During the day, that sort of thing took place with lightning speed. My anorak was so long that when I squatted down, it was almost like a tent, which saved me from the worst of the wind. Nonetheless, after these minor stops, I had to move as fast as I could for ten or fifteen minutes to thaw out and bring warmth back again.

I didn't want to interfere with nature by taking pills to prevent menstruation. Experience had taught me that it would be stopped anyway by severe effort, and this indeed turned out to be the case.

The deep cold and clean air meant that I never felt dirty, but I was soaked with sweat, so every day I indulged in one moist wipe. I normally didn't miss a shower. But if you have no shower, you learn to accept the fact. Eventually my skin became nice and soft, and I felt that it was actually benefiting by the rest from daily showers. Presumably, we civilized human beings bathe and shower too much, thus washing natural oils out of the skin.

Eating so much sweet food as I did, I really looked forward to brushing my teeth every day, morning and evening. On the move, my daily rations consisted of a whole slab of Stratos aerated chocolate with nuts, sweet biscuits, marzipan, and sweet drinks.

For lunch, I ate a new cereal product I was testing. Dinner consisted of freeze-dried food. The menu was spaghetti, meat, and rice, reconstituted in boiling water. While the Primus was roaring, I served the hors d'oeuvre, which was always the same: crushed, vacuum-packed potato chips without salt, varied with a few spices that I carried. I always saved a little XL-1 in a thermos so that I had something to drink with it. I also had a few bags of strongly flavored sweets, especially licorice.

I'M ENJOYING MYSELF!

On my expedition, I never actually experienced the horrors caused by hunger, cold, and bad equipment that had featured so prominently in the polar literature I'd read. It's hardly surprising that the heroes of yesteryear had a rough time of it. They were faced with unfamiliar conditions and didn't always have the suitable equipment that is available to modern expeditions. For example, we have light sleeping bags filled with down; they had to make do with heavy ones made of fur, which soaked up dampness like a sponge and could never really be dried. Food didn't provide enough calories. Footgear could be problematic. Scott's second expedition, for example, suffered horribly frostbitten feet, and their boots were not nearly as good as mine. Amundsen's boots turned out to be too small at first, so his feet froze. He and his companions had to modify their boots four times before they finally started on the polar journey.

On the early part of his trek, Amundsen was dressed in sealskin outer garments over woolen underclothes. This is appropriate if, like Amundsen at that stage, one sits on a sled for much of the time and doesn't sweat, while the dogs do all the work. Had I been dressed that way, I would have collapsed with heat stroke.

Sealskin aside, the fundamentals of dressing for the cold remain about the same as they've always been. They're based on the layering principle, with plenty of space between layers to allow air circulation. Modern clothing, however, is generally lighter, and new methods of weaving mean that windproof garments breathe

A single day without a face mask caused several spots of frostbite. After that I took care to wear a mask every day.

better and woolen underclothes provide better insulation. I would have had no objection to taking a pure cotton anorak on the expedition but chose microfiber instead, because it's lighter in weight and dries more quickly. All in all, there's no question that modern expeditions, eschewing dogs and depots along the route, are more athletic performances than anything else.

The English have suffered the most in the snows. The misery they have experienced is beyond belief, especially since it was mostly self-inflicted, with poor food and dismal equipment. Both Shackleton and Scott visited Norway, but they ignored, or at most followed half-heartedly, the advice given them by Amundsen and Nansen to use skis and dogs and to dress like the Eskimos. Had they listened to the Norwegians, the English might have conquered the South Pole by 1903, during Scott's first expedition. The tales from their Antarctic enterprises are enough to frighten off anyone from even considering these inhospitable regions.

I often thought of Amundsen, Shackleton, and Scott, and with the sufferings of the old heroes at the back of my mind, I tramped on toward the south. I had enough food as well as proven equipment and navigational systems. I had prepared myself mentally in advance by assuming that conditions would be horribly cold and unpleasant. I had absorbed all the sufferings of the old polar explorers into my subconscious, where they were churned over for many years. Psychologically, I was prepared for my own expedition to turn out just as badly. But on several occasions I had to stop and say to myself, "But now I'm here and it's—quite fantastic!" I didn't need to pinch myself in order to realize I was really in the Antarctic on my way to the South Pole rather than only dreaming. The wind quickly performed that service by cutting through to the marrow of my bones whenever I stopped. What happened to the suffering? Of course it was cold, but I was expecting it to be colder. It began to dawn on me that I was on the ski tour of my life.

I took care to follow the routine I had worked out before I started, especially in making and breaking camp. In addition to my stove, fuel bottles, cooker, sleeping bag, and mats, I took into the tent with me a special bag containing food for three days, plastic bottles with powdered drinks, tool kit, GPS, map, diary, and other necessary items. I was meticulous about maintaining the proper level of food in this tent bag. Once only did I have to dress and go outside to unpack the sled and fetch food after I had lit the Primus—a cold job indeed. There was no one to help me pitch the tent or light the Primus if I was too cold. Therefore, I promised myself to make camp the moment I felt the least sign of freezing. On five separate occasions, I stopped earlier than intended, either because of rising wind or because of exhaustion and cold.

After two weeks, I was sleeping soundly and waking just before half past six every morning without an alarm clock. At almost exactly 6:30 a.m. I was out of my sleeping bag. The time varied by only a few minutes from day to day. I ate breakfast, packed up, and at 8:30 a.m. was ready for the day's grind.

Depending on the force of the wind, packing the sled might mean a few horrible minutes of being frozen to the marrow. Even while wearing a down jacket, I felt the insidious cold creep in.

Each time I went out with a load to the sled, I had to close it securely before going back into the tent for more. All this took time.

I had no desire whatsoever to make things harder by losing my tent, sleeping bags, or mats. I learned my lesson in the course of the first week, when I lost two thermos cups during rest stops. On the one occasion, I put the cup down in my lee, out of the wind; on the other, it was between my boots. Thoroughgoing squalls left me with just one cup. I improvised a spare from a funnel, and never did I let the last proper cup out of my grasp during a rest.

Once, a ski pole was also in the process of being blown away, but I hurled myself after it and was able to grab hold of it. After that, I took the precaution of always pushing my ski poles under the straps on the sled during a rest stop.

Whenever I had to take off my face mask or a mitten in order to do something, the wind felt like the blows of a lash on my skin and my fingertips were immediately seized by the cold. I swung my arms for all I was worth before my nails began to ache, and thus warmth came flowing back.

The worst moment of the day was when the sled was finally packed and I had to take off my down jacket, stuff it into my rucksack, harness myself to the sled, rig the compass mounting on my belt, and, last of all, put on my skis. Since I was thinly clad for moving, not standing still, the wind cut to the bone before I got going. Now and then it was so cold that I nearly began to whine, behaving like a racehorse at the starting gate, kicking and stamping, raring to go. It was a heavenly feeling when the warmth gradually began to flow through my veins.

Even though I knew that some freezing-cold moments awaited me outside before I could be warm again, I was never tempted to stay in my sleeping bag when I woke up. I looked forward to each day. I felt the thrill of anticipation when considering how the day would turn out, what kind of wind and weather

I might face, how big the sastrugi would be, how far I would manage to advance, and what kind of thoughts would keep me company.

Regularly, every hour, I would stop, sit down on the sled, and eat a piece of chocolate, a biscuit, or a little marzipan and, above all, drink something. At two o'clock I stopped for lunch, a hot meal eaten out of the widemouthed food thermos. The rest stops weren't quite as desperately cold as my preparation time in the morning, but not far off. If it was blowing too hard, I didn't sit down on the sled but stood with my back to the wind. I barely gave the food time to settle before starting off again. After each break, I concentrated exclusively on working up warmth again.

MESSAGE NO. 6:
"FINISH SOUTH POLE"

I had an arrangement to call the base at Patriot Hills every Thursday at 8:30 a.m. or, if I couldn't make contact, to try again at 10:30 a.m. I didn't quite understand what I had done wrong, but the radio refused to work. I never made contact.

After three weeks, I gave up trying, banished the radio to the bottom of the sled, and tried to forget the useless eight extra kilos I was hauling. Had it only been eight kilos of marzipan! I considered dumping the radio in a crevasse, but I had borrowed it, and it was worth the best part of $29,000. Besides, one does not pollute the Antarctic.

I was well aware that I wasn't supposed to leave anything behind and carried all refuse that couldn't be burned. Even though nobody had ever trod my path before, compared with the old heroes, I was no discoverer but only a glorified tourist, here for my own pleasure, and tourists ought to be careful in untouched country.

For people in search of peace and quiet and extraordinary experience, the Arctic and Antarctic have become popular destinations. Most visitors are interested exclusively in landscape and animal life. They often arrive as passengers on cruise ships, observe animals and scenery from the deck, or land on prepared sites. The tour operators are as a rule perfectly aware that they ought to respect the wilderness, and since these tours are relatively expensive, there's no question of mass tourism, at least in the immediate future. Personally, I don't believe that organized tourism will destroy any of these sites. On Svalbard, I've noticed that those who are keenest on strict preservation are precisely those who have managed to experience that fantastic landscape outside the authorized tourist sites. Scientists, too, are often critical of tourists, but in both the Arctic and the Antarctic these researchers are demonstrably by far the greater environmental sinners.

At home, followers of my expedition would certainly be disappointed at having no news from the Antarctic. I hadn't particularly looked forward to these weekly reports, even though I had decided in advance on the subjects I was to deal with on the way. Many of my thoughts were highly personal and difficult to convey coherently during a short transmission. Anyway, the Norwegian P4 radio channel was certainly hoping for some drama, but my reports would have borne a closer resemblance to "News from Nowhere."

As things were, I was spared the necessity of thinking in a structured way. I could let my thoughts run freely. That the radio refused to work came as a relief; I didn't feel a need to send reports or talk to anyone. I had brought along a video camera, with the intention of filming my weekly broadcasts. *National Geographic* magazine had been interested in a film but withdrew just before I departed. I wasn't exactly brimming over with enthusiasm when I took out the camera, a fact reflected in the footage. For the most part, I seemed to have filmed the iris of one eye. Evidently, I didn't have full mastery of the zoom button. It was rather hopeless and chiefly of interest to ophthalmic specialists, I thought.

At home, my press agent, Wanda Widerøe, had to eke out press reports as best she could from the scant information I sent via the Argos transmitter. We went through the expedition thoroughly before I departed, and I felt we were on the same wavelength even without radio contact. She knew precisely how I would react in given circumstances, and in any case, so far there had been no great surprises to report.

The Argos radio worked with prearranged message codes, of which I had fifteen. I switched it on every evening at seven o'clock. The transmission went via satellite to Toulouse, France, and was then relayed to *Aftenposten,* the big daily newspaper in Oslo, where it was sent on to Einar's and Wanda's pagers. They would have my position and message code the following day.

The Argos transmitter was supposed to report the temperature but instead reported a constant value of 88 degrees Celsius (190 degrees Fahrenheit). It was so outlandish that no one was fooled. I knew that Einar was most concerned about crevasses. It was just as well that he didn't know how many there were and that I had come in close contact with a few.

The message I transmitted almost daily was simply a zero, which stood for "Everything OK." I used it even if there was wind and driving snow. I had decided to send the fewest negative reports I could get away with. It was only in the third week of my journey that I sent message no. 4, "Poor Weather." The day began with a gale, and I made camp in a squall. At home, they would see by my position from the Argos transmitter that I had only advanced four kilometers that day and might perhaps imagine that I was in a crevassed area if I sent a zero.

Some messages concerned weather and snow conditions. Four were reserved for emergencies, like no. 13: "Want Immediate Pickup." Message no. 8 was a private one to Einar. I only used no. 15, "Merry Christmas/Happy Birthday," on two occasions: on Einar's birthday and on Christmas Eve.

At a certain point I discovered that I hadn't screwed the antenna on properly. The threads were worn out. I knew that the Argos transmitter had worked at Punta Arenas and on the first day at Patriot Hills. How long had the antenna rattled in the screw thread? I was worried about those at home: had they received any messages at all?

We had agreed that if no messages were received, a rescue operation was not to be launched before my planned date of arrival at the South Pole. The greatest dangers were falling into crevasses or freezing to death if I were injured in some other way. We all agreed that the probability of the Argos transmitter failing was greater than that of my having an accident. It was convenient for me: either I was on my way—or frozen to death. But now I understood that after more than a month's uncertainty, it might be trying for those at home.

I had a plan known only to a select few. I proposed to turn around at the South Pole and ski-sail back to Patriot Hills. An extra sled—waiting at Patriot Hills with food and fuel for forty days and an Up-Ski parachute—was to be flown in to the South Pole at the end of November.

Patriot Hills would be closing for the season on January 24. If I didn't return by then, I would have to charter an aircraft from Punta Arenas, at a cost of more than $200,000. To arrive in time, I would have to keep up a good speed with the help of the parachute. After three weeks on my expedition, I understood it would be too dangerous, if not impossible, to ski-sail over the huge sastrugi. I transmitted message no. 6: "FS. Finish South Pole."

I was bitterly disappointed. My whole plan was based on sailing back. It would have been fun to manage the South Pole and back on my own. Since I knew so little about the conditions along the route I had chosen, I thought it was sensible to delay revealing this plan before I was on the spot. Now I was devoutly grateful that I had done so. I thought about how thin the line was dividing success from failure and how careful one had to be in dealing with the press and their manner of handling information. Had I talked beforehand about my plan to do the round trip, the headlines around Christmas would definitely have been different.

After making the decision, I had plenty of time for the remainder of the trip. During the past few weeks, I had seen that it was possible to reach the South Pole by December 21. I remembered that ANI had a flight out around that time, and I was afraid that they'd want me on it.

I had dreamed of the South Pole for so long and wasn't at all eager to arrive only to be bundled into a plane the next moment and flown out. I was looking forward to a few quiet days at the South Pole, with time to absorb all the impressions and get my thoughts in order. I decided to arrive on Christmas Eve, as the Christmas gift of my life.

AND THE SATELLITES
KEEP ORBITING

What I had learned in my days of orienteering was of little use in the Antarctic, since a map is no help in those huge, featureless white spaces. I did look at the map in the tent, however, and mark off how far I had gone. I took it out every evening when I lay in my sleeping bag, warm, well fed, and comfortable—a little ritual.

I navigated by satellite, using GPS, which was originally established by the Americans for military purposes, among other things to enable submarines and ships to find their precise position when they surfaced. Thanks to the U.S. Congress, civilians can use the system, too. Politicians realized that the cost of developing the system—twelve billion dollars—was enough to warrant wider clientele access to its benefits. All aircraft now navigate by GPS, and when used for mapping, it's accurate to about five centimeters (two inches). The system depends on twenty-four satellites orbiting the earth at an altitude of 20,000 kilometers (12,500 miles). In my case, to find my position, I needed contact with three satellites—four to determine my altitude. I could find my position within fifteen meters (fifty feet).

In the old days, polar navigation was accomplished by determining the altitude of the sun. Amundsen used a sextant and Scott a theodolite to take the observations, followed by tedious calculations with pencil and paper. Satellites have made it much

In a whiteout with no point of reference, I skied staring at the compass. Otherwise, I navigated by the shadow of the sun and the direction of the sastrugi.

easier to be a polar traveler. The GPS that I was using was no bigger than a pocket calculator. It did, however, depend on batteries, and before departure, I spent a lot of time having the correct leads made for connecting to a lithium battery—necessary in the low Antarctic temperatures.

One of the high points of the day came after I had taken off my outer garments, scraped the ice and brushed the snow off my clothes, and lit the Primus. While the snow melted for dinner, I took out the GPS and pressed a button, and after a minute or two, it had locked on to enough satellites to fix my position and altitude precisely. With simple programming, it could also tell me how far I had traveled in the course of the day and give me the next day's course. It also indicated the compass deviation.

I had two satellite navigators. Even if both failed, I could still navigate by the aid of a compass, a watch, and the sun, but it wouldn't be precise. Should worse come to worst, I would also alter course farther west, so that I would eventually be able to see the Hercules aircraft that shuttle all summer between the South Pole and the base at McMurdo Sound.

To begin with, it was strange to see the sun move counterclockwise down there, which is the opposite of what one is used to in the Northern Hemisphere. I started by setting a course for three summits called Three Sails. After they disappeared, I had the Ellsworth Mountains behind me for a few days, with high nunataks on the western horizon. Partly due to bad weather and an undulating landscape, I didn't see the Thiel Mountains to the west, a marker I expected to see at the halfway point. I was somewhat uncertain but preferred to trust my GPS and the sun. Suddenly, one morning, I saw the mountains on the horizon behind me and could confirm that I was where I believed I was and where the satellite navigator indicated.

To steer a course during the day, I had fixed my compass on a mounting attached to my belt. At high latitudes, however,

Day 4. The Three Sails mountains in the background helped me hold direction for many days.

the magnetic compass displays certain peculiarities. The earth acts like a giant magnet, and the needle of the compass points to its poles. The red part of the needle points north, the other south. In the Antarctic, however, the North Magnetic Pole is so far away, and its attraction so weak, that the south-seeking end of the compass needle is dragged down, with a risk of jamming against the casing. To balance this, a small weight is usually attached to the red end of the needle.

The magnetic poles are some distance from the geographic poles. Consequently, the compass rarely points to true north or south but deviates by amounts that vary according to position and that are appreciable near the poles. Along my route, the deviation was for the most part around 40 degrees, which I naturally had to allow for in steering. To make things more complicated, the earth's magnetic field is constantly changing. In 1907–8, when Shackleton's expedition first reached the South Magnetic Pole, the magnetic field lay in South Victoria Land; now it's out to sea between McMurdo Sound and New Zealand!

Because of wind and sastrugi, I strayed a little off course every day, but thanks to the satellite navigator, I could make the necessary correction each morning. I had plenty of time in the mornings. It was lovely: no stress, no fuss, no bother. Nonetheless, I continued to awaken each day as if my alarm clock were set for half past six. I had taken the clock in case I had difficulty adjusting to round-the-clock light, with no distinction between night and day, but I never needed it. In fact, I enjoyed myself immensely in the mornings, drinking a large cup of coffee, lying lazily, half-dressed, on top of my sleeping bag. I did nothing, just lay and let my thoughts drift by. I thought of all the people struggling to get up in the autumnal gloom at home, sitting in traffic jams, standing in crowded buses and trams. I nearly felt a touch of guilt.

A QUIET TOAST HALFWAY

On November 30, I crossed 85° south latitude and was at the halfway mark. I had been underway for twenty-five days, and my plan to arrive on Christmas Eve seemed realistic.

At lunchtime, when I assumed I had crossed the magic parallel, I stopped and unharnessed myself from the sled. I circled it at a distance of 500 meters (550 yards) while following the horizon with my eyes. It was white and blue and white and blue as far as I could see. I twisted and turned, and the white expanses ran on to eternity.

The South Pole was 600 kilometers (375 miles) away; so was Patriot Hills. I was at the point of no return. If I tripped on a sastrugi and broke a leg or fell into a crevasse, there would be little chance of coming back alive. Admittedly, I had an emergency transmitter in my backpack, but I knew quite well that it gave a false sense of security. I would almost certainly freeze to death before help arrived. I dredged up various horrific images to arouse my deepest feelings. I knew I would never again be so alone in such a deserted place. I tried to examine my thoughts carefully: was I frightened, had I discovered something new about myself, was I in touch with higher powers? I felt no anxiety but noticed considerable tension in my body. What I felt above all was peace of mind. I had never felt calmer or more secure. I felt intensely alive. It was immensely satisfying to achieve what I'd believed possible.

I could depend only on myself. Everyone says it's safe to be

My journal was a good communication partner.

a polar explorer these days—in an emergency, all you have to do is turn on the direction-finding radio and help will come. That's assuming it's flying weather, that you're not lying jammed in a crevasse, and that you're conscious.

As the days turned into weeks, I felt that the open spaces, wind, and weather had begun controlling me, setting my natural rhythm. I felt a powerful communion with nature, with the weather, as if I was a natural part of the whole. I felt it must have been a religious experience in its true sense. The word "religion" derives from the Latin word *religare*, a compound of *re*, meaning "back," and *ligare*, "to bind": in other words, "that which binds one back." I can understand religion if it means leading people back into contact with their origins.

Many polar explorers have written of a strong feeling that God, or some outside being, was present, almost like a guardian angel. I didn't feel that a Creator was behind what I felt, but that might have had something to do with what I was taught as a child. All people and all cultures have their own conceptions of who or what God is. In Norway we are taught to conceive of God as a male. At primary school and Sunday school, He is even described as a man with a white beard, sitting on a cloud, surrounded by angels—at least that was the case when I was a child. He noted all your naughtiness, but if you behaved, you would go where He was. We Norwegians are automatically born into the state church; I contracted out at an early age.

I feel more in common with those who declare religion to be a link between one's body and soul and the rest of the universe. If the purpose of religion is to bring the individual into harmony with the laws of nature and to teach people to appreciate true values, which all are given the opportunity to seek, then I believe that religion is a good thing, something we need. But as far as I'm concerned, religion has nothing to do with the worship of God, ritual, or racial conflict; it's about the individual, nature, and the universe all being in tune.

When I had to make a decision, I tried to listen to my feelings—for example, in the crevasse area at the beginning and also when something told me that it was time to make camp, even if I hadn't completed the planned ten-hour march. If I followed my intuition, everything seemed in tune. As soon as I succumbed to argument or defiance, the pleasant feelings vanished.

The first time I ignored intuition was after one week in Antarctica. I awoke to a heavy gale but thought, *There is no bad weather, only bad clothing.* My equipment was in order, so I set off. After an hour, I recognized that I ought to have stayed in the tent, which had been my first thought when I woke up and looked at the weather. Snow was driving hard, while the wind continued to increase. I carried on for another hour, hoping the wind would drop, but it blew even harder, and finally I decided to make camp. I hesitated a bit, dreading having to unpack the sled. Pitching the tent in that kind of wind would be a horribly cold and difficult job. I was somewhat anxious; if anything blew away, I would be in a critical position. There was something ominous about the whole situation. I felt somehow on the edge of survival, but at least it made me concentrate fully. It took a long time to pitch the tent, more than half an hour; usually it was up in a few minutes. I promised myself never again to argue with my initial gut feeling.

As I continued on my way, I made more and more contact with my intuition, or perhaps simply with myself. Intuition is one of the most fantastic qualities we are given, and perhaps we ignore it too much in everyday life. If we ignore our innermost feelings often enough, we lose something of ourselves.

After circling the sled at the halfway point, I returned to it, took off my down jacket, harnessed up, and continued on. It was the first time in twenty-five days that I had moved so much without the sled, and I felt incredibly free and unencumbered. Now I felt how heavy that sled was; in fact, it seemed heavier than when I had started down the ice shelf. This was hardly surprising: it had snowed during the night, and five centimeters (two inches) of fresh-fallen flakes in deep cold were rough, clingy, and an effective brake. But the weather was fine again, with clear skies. The sun was shining, and a light breeze was blowing. I went on for another five hours before making camp.

Since I was halfway, I allowed myself something extra that evening. My supplies included a little bottle of Drambuie, and after dinner I indulged in a small glass (well, actually, a film container) and my mother's Kentucky cake as an accompaniment to my coffee. While every Saturday I allowed myself a piece of cake with coffee, the Drambuie was reserved for three occasions: Einar's birthday, the halfway point, and Christmas Eve. These were the only times when I missed company. It's no fun to *skol* with yourself. The potent liqueur tasted like 90-proof distilled spirits.

I had brought along a good cigar for Christmas Eve. I checked its condition now, presumably because I wanted a secret puff or two. To my horror, I saw that it lay shattered in a thousand pieces. Evidently the toolbox in which I had lovingly enclosed it for protection must have received a blow. I tried repairing the damage with toilet paper, but I had to give up in the end.

Before I left home, Wanda had given me a letter, with strict instructions that it was not to be opened before I was well on my way. She had approved of the expedition from the moment she first heard of it and had given me enormous encouragement and support. Halfway surely qualified as a fine time to read the letter, so I took it out and reverently opened it. It had been a long time since the postman was in the vicinity, and it was inspiring to have a letter to read so far away from home. Besides a delightful letter, the envelope contained poetry and quotations. I was a little intoxicated by the liquid dietary additive, and as a result I found it difficult to sleep. I wrote a few extra pages in my diary and indulged in a little homesickness. I read the poetry that Wanda sent before I finally fell asleep.

I also had Ibsen's *Peer Gynt* as reading material and a selection of rhythmic and modern Norwegian poetry (which, to save weight, I had cut out, pasted together, and reduced in size on a photocopier). Some of the poems had themes from nature, while others were social criticism.

On some of my previous long tours, I had been so exhausted during the afternoons that coherent thought was no longer in working order. At that point, melodies like "Lambada" started hammering in my head. Anyone who has experienced something similar will know that it's not particularly uplifting to hum "Lambada" incessantly for days on end.

It had been years since I'd had the time to read poetry, and on this trip I had looked forward to doing so. My idea was that, during the afternoons, when I was becoming exhausted, I would think of what I had read the previous evening. It worked brilliantly; it was only during the past few days that my concentration had begun to fail.

I also wanted to use my reading as a kind of mantra, in case I was overcome by angst or gloomy thoughts—hence, *Peer Gynt,* a metrical verse drama and practically the Norwegian national epic poem. I proposed to learn the more rhythmic passages by heart and absorb the imagery. In this way, I imagined, I could steer my thoughts away from the depressing side of things if such appeared. *Peer* returned home, unread.

At the outset, when I was mentally exhausted, I memorized a poem called "Stillheten Etterpå" (The Silence That Follows), by Rolf Jacobsen, a modern Norwegian poet. That suited my state of mind. Another of his works that cropped up was "Fjell" (Mountains), a poem that puts things in perspective and reminds us of our allotted time on earth. We must use every day while we are here.

I OWN A COUNTRY OF THE HEART THAT NO ONE ELSE CAN TOUCH

I was often possessed by thoughts of life and death during the first few weeks, when I had many hard days. In Punta Arenas, I suffered the strongest reaction to having suppressed Berit's tragedy. On All Saints' Day, we went to the churchyard to look at all the flowers that had replaced our sleds on the flight. The pictures of the dead, flowers, and candles released a violent reaction. I stumbled out, dissolving in tears, and made my way to an unknown part of the town. I don't know how long I wandered around there, but I was completely broken down. I went through the poor quarters, looked down at the edge of the sea, and took an ice-cold plunge in the Strait of Magellan. I thought of Magellan, killed in the Philippines during his circumnavigation of the globe. He left his mark. So did Berit, who was such an inspiration to others.

Gradually, such thoughts were replaced by other existential ones that I would mull over for hours at a time. For example, I often wondered what I would be when I grew up and what I would do when I came home. For thirteen years, interrupted by leaves of absence, I'd been a teacher. I had a degree that included courses in Norwegian language and literature, history, gymnastics, and counseling. I had left my teaching job three years earlier, and now (once more) I had a leave of absence from Svalbard Polar Travel. I missed the teaching and contact with my students but never the piles of compositions to correct. I was constantly being asked when I was going to settle down. For my part, I felt quite at ease, but the hunger for new adventures was always there. Perhaps I would find true peace of mind when I had reached the South Pole. I thought of the trips to Greenland and Svalbard that Einar and I had dreamed about. When I first met him, he had little taste for tent life when the temperature was far below zero, but now he was beginning to see the light. Perhaps there might be another crossing of Greenland, together with him this time. In any case, I couldn't conceive of a quiet domestic life and would undoubtedly seize any opportunity to go on new adventures.

When I was nineteen years old, I wrote CARPE DIEM on my cap when I enrolled in college; there was surely no reason to stop seizing opportunity even after I had passed my fortieth birthday. If I could keep healthy, the possibilities were many. Thus I brooded and philosophized as I pushed on southward.

The hardest times in the Antarctic were the whiteouts. This is a state in which clouds, fog, or falling snow diffuses the light in such a way that all contours vanish, everything is planed out into a monotonous white, and earth and sky melt confusingly into one. It's impossible to see the horizon or the sastrugi, and consequently there is a disturbing sense of disorientation. I would stumble and fall among the sastrugi. The sled would stop dead or overturn. Then I would have to control my thoughts and dredge up images: I would imagine the road where I had hauled car tires the previous autumn and go over my training circuit near my home, every stream, every pebble and tree stump along the path, every viewpoint.

If I had difficulties steering my thoughts in a positive direction, I used the words of another Norwegian poet, Nordahl Grieg, as a mantra:

I own a country of the heart
that no one else can touch
Hill rises upon hill
in the heavy forest calm.

Eventually, images of mountain and forest rose up. I had to laugh at myself. There I was, struggling along on skis in a sea of white while actually dreaming of skiing, admittedly with lightweight equipment on manicured tracks at home.

Some days I moved in a kind of meditative condition. When I took out my diary on those occasions, it was difficult to put anything on paper. I couldn't remember any particular thoughts or events during the day but could only note huge reserves of energy. Nor was I especially hungry or thirsty on those days. Presumably, I spent much less energy than if I had been struggling with gloomy thoughts or had allowed myself to be irritated by the sastrugi or the wind. I have also experienced a state of meditation at home while running. I would suddenly be back at the car, though my watch showed that I had been running for an hour. I couldn't remember where I'd been, although it was probably the same circuit I had always run year after year.

By nature, I'm not a fatalist. I always believe that everything will turn out well and that "it will be all right on the night." I never thought I would come to any harm in Antarctica, but during my preparations before departure it was nonetheless important to visualize accidents that might happen and, as far as possible, conceive of how they could be avoided. As the years have passed, I've become more and more conscious of how we are driven by our thoughts. We are what we think.

I prepared myself mentally to tackle all conceivable difficulties and imagined what I would do in various situations. What probably concerned me most was how I would react in a critical situation, given that I would be absolutely on my own: would I be paralyzed by angst and behave irrationally? I had never actually experienced the angst that paralyzes a person or causes panic, but I had felt what it was like to be anxious. After escaping relatively unharmed from an avalanche, I was left with a kind of phobia.

At Høgevarde, on Norefjell, a skiing area near Oslo, a companion once triggered a slab avalanche that buried me in snow. I tried to do what I had learned, to ski diagonally out of the path of the avalanche, but the snow packed itself around my skis and dragged me down. Most frightening were the huge slabs of snow that bore down on me, and episodes from my childhood passed rapidly before my eyes in full color, episodes I had never before remembered or thought about. I managed to hold a ski pole high above my head; my companions followed the orange basket and were soon by my side when the avalanche had stopped.

After that I had a phobia of small, enclosed spaces and big crowds. Anxiety would arise abruptly. Once, when I was in a crowded elevator, I suddenly began sweating and had difficulty breathing. I immediately understood why and concentrated on breathing calmly and talking reassuringly to myself. Following that experience, I rode on elevators as often as possible and deliberately buried myself in big crowds until I conquered the fear. Years may pass before I have another attack, but it can still descend suddenly and unpredictably. I've learned how to control the reaction.

My reaction to angst is essentially positive and might perhaps best be called excitement. It's a sensation that focuses my energy both physically and mentally, both while skiing on glaciers and when climbing. Competition gives me a little of the same feeling.

One American study asked subjects to describe situations in which they had felt happiest and to state which emotions besides happiness were present. In many cases, that other emotion was a degree of anxiety, not too strong and not too weak. What we remember as happiness is often a situation in which there's tension as well. It might be when we try something new—a new job or relationship, for example. We have to bear a little angst in order to advance. It's important to accept this and not try to evade it.

Many people live as if they haven't chosen their way of life. They accommodate themselves as if they're unable to do anything about it. They stay in a safety zone, continuing to live with their frustrations, in the belief that this is what life must be. One principle adopted by many people, but that can easily become a cocoon, is "Better the devil you know than the devil you don't." And so they remain in jobs they dislike and in relationships that no longer function, all for fear of anything new. Fear is meant to be conquered.

HIGH SASTRUGI AND DEEP CREVASSES

One-third of the way to the South Pole, I now faced the hardest part of the journey. Having passed the Thiel Mountains, I was at an altitude of 1,300 meters (4,200 feet) above sea level, but over the next few days I was to climb another 1,500 meters (4,900 feet). Up in the heights, it became colder and the snow got even more clingy and abrasive. The air was also thinner, but since I had been climbing slowly, I was at any rate well acclimated.

Near the Pole, the atmosphere contains appreciably less oxygen. The South Pole lies 2,850 meters (9,300 feet) above sea level, but the true oxygen content of the atmosphere is equivalent to an altitude of 4,000 meters (13,000 feet) closer to the equator.

Visibility returned after a couple of days of whiteout, and I could now see the polar plateau rising toward the south. The terrain was undulating, and it was hard work dragging my sled upward. Now and then, I encountered gentle downhill slopes, but because of the abrasive snow and the skins on my skis, there was no relief, and I had to continue tramping and hauling as before. The sled didn't feel any lighter, despite my having eaten and used up fuel for more than twenty-five days. The sled was twenty-five kilos (fifty-five pounds) lighter, but I didn't notice it.

It had snowed during the past few days. I examined the sled, believing that ice had formed on the runners. It felt as if I was hauling a sled with chains, but the runners were actually just as smooth as when I started. In Greenland, I had attempted to improve the glide of the sled in the Eskimo manner, by coating the runners with water, which froze into a thin layer of ice. Perhaps it worked on wooden runners but not on the plastic from which modern runners are made.

Amundsen once described Antarctic snow as "fish glue." All too true, alas. The landscape was far more undulating than I had imagined. It climbed in a succession of rounded steps with ridges and gentle hollows, exactly as on the uplands at home in Norway.

For a few days, I had been considering whether I ought to keep the course I had set at the beginning and had since been following. This was due south along the meridian of 80°30′ west. The map on which I was marking my track dated back to 1975. According to this, about two weeks earlier I ought to have passed two nunataks along my course. I never saw hide nor hair of either. At 87° south, the map indicated a crevassed area. Over the whole journey, I actually encountered five large crevassed areas, although according to the map there were only two.

Despite the fact that I was on a huge ice stream, it was surprising that the crevasses were so exposed. I received an explanation at the South Pole. Little snow had fallen during the previous winter. The crevasses had always been there, but wind and sun had eaten away at the snow covering, now making them visible. The sun had also melted the snow next to the edge of the crevasses on the snow bridges. If the same pilots had mapped the whole area, they might have mistaken the crevasses, and not only the nunataks. Therefore, I kept the same course.

It was a horribly cold morning, and I started off like a maniac to work up some warmth. I had to climb up the steep side of a ridge, which I could see was going to be difficult. It was a long way, and I was prepared for the struggle ahead, but not for any drama.

The previous day, I had seen this ridge in the distance. It

came closer and closer, and at the end of the day I made camp at its foot. It wasn't a typical "zebra ridge," striped with crevasses. In fact, I didn't notice a single crevasse. The only thing that distinguished this particular ridge was that it seemed longer and steeper than any other slope I had climbed so far. I was prepared for crevasses on top because of the stresses in the ice. After a while it became so steep that I could no longer manage to ski straight up. My skis began slipping backward, so I started zigzagging across the slope. As on all slopes exposed to the sun, the snow was mostly in the form of crust. In between, there were patches of drift snow, but I followed the fields of crust, across which it was easiest to move. When the slope became so steep that the sled protested, I took off my skis, put them on the sled, and walked straight up with the help of my ski poles.

Apart from some cracks a few centimeters wide, I didn't notice anything untoward until I suddenly fell through up to my hips. As if by reflex, I hurled myself backward. The sled slid backward, too, and gave me a little tug out of the hole, but I lost my balance, and one of my ski poles broke through into the crevasse, releasing a minor avalanche. I stared down into the blue-tinted depths.

Leaning back, I hauled myself up by one hand with the aid of the rope harnessing me to the sled. In a few seconds I was out of the hole. I went back to the sled, put on my skis again, and crossed the crevasse safely a few meters away from the hole. With my skis on, I felt safe. I kept them on for the rest of the day, and didn't dwell on what had happened.

I was a little anxious when I had to take off my skis to make camp. In the tent, I took out the map and saw that I was a day's march from the crevasses I had previously noticed. Therefore, I changed course slightly to the west, in case the map was right after all.

The reaction arrived during the night. I had a nightmare in which the whole camp—tent, sled, and myself in the sleeping bag—dropped down into a bottomless chasm. I woke with a feeling of claustrophobia, deep down in my sleeping bag. Thereafter, I examined camping sites even more carefully than before. I was somewhat annoyed with myself for a few days because of what had happened. I had known that I was moving over a large ice stream, and the fact that the crevasses were open on the ridges I had seen in the distance had made me careless. A steep slope on an ice stream means that the ice is under strain, which in turn means that crevasses are likely. The blue depths that opened under me after I broke through gave me a horrible shock, even though my sled and rucksack acted like anchors, precisely as I had anticipated in case of an accident.

The change of course turned out to be sensible. The following day, I saw a large area with open crevasses to the east. I was on the outskirts and crossed a dozen crevasses, but these were much narrower than the ones I could see in the distance. Those I encountered were between two and five meters (six to fifteen feet) across. The ends of the snow bridges were rotten, so I crept over in Pink Panther style again. I encountered traces of surveying, in the shape of bamboo poles put out to measure the speed of the ice stream, and retracted my mistrust of those who had mapped the area.

A few days later, I entered a region with sastrugi up to two meters high, impossible to negotiate on skis. When I sank a few centimeters into the drift snow, I gave a start. I hadn't forgotten the crevasse that I had nearly fallen into and the blue depths beneath. I felt unsafe without skis and was constantly on my guard. Afterward, I observed that on these days of grinding toil and profound concentration, the entries in my diary were extremely laconic, just a line or two. Such days were exhausting, with no opportunity for flights of fancy or philosophizing.

The sastrugi didn't cease and were bigger than expected. It was a real grind to cross them. In all, I traveled 800 kilometers

(500 miles) through high sastrugi, more than half the distance. Eventually, I developed a special technique for surmounting them. I hauled for all I was worth to get the sled to the top, and once it was over, I ran a few steps to avoid being overtaken and struck in the heel by it. Whether I liked it or not, occasionally I had to take off my skis to get across. I felt decidedly unsafe without skis; the two episodes in which I had broken through the surface always remained at the back of my mind.

The first few days among the sastrugi were reasonable enough, but I was confounded as time passed and the terrain remained like a stormy sea. I remembered the Italian mountaineer Reinholdt Messner's description of his journey to the South Pole. I had thought he was exaggerating, since his whole book was one long chronicle of suffering. His route diverged somewhat from mine, but he did describe enormous sastrugi, especially after the Thiel Mountains.

To begin with, I was irritated by not being able to remove my skins. They increased the friction on the already rough snow, but without them, I wouldn't have had enough grip to haul my sled over the sastrugi. When all was said and done, skins were preferable to clambering up sideways or doing herringbones day after day. I wondered how Cato was doing. There must have been sastrugi in his path as well. I could scarcely imagine how he would manage to overcome them without arms or poles to help him.

Finally, I accepted that such was the terrain and there was nothing to be done about it. If I were to curse every sastruga along the way, it wouldn't be an enjoyable trip. Far better to consider what was admirable in the formations. Even if the sastrugi definitely made the journey harder, they had a beauty of their own: the most unbelievable shapes and many beautiful shades of blue. It was like going through an art gallery of modern sculpture that was miles long. It inspired thoughts and imagination.

As the days and weeks passed, I had overcome everything

that had so exhausted me before I set off. A powerful sense of communion with nature felt reassuring. I was inspired by nature's works of art and felt my mental energy rising.

December 14 marked eighty-three years since Roald Amundsen attained the South Pole, and that evening I had planned a little celebration in his honor. That day turned out to be the hardest of the whole journey. During the night, a storm swept down, and I slept badly as the wind tore at the tent, making it tremble and flap. During the past week, I had passed thousands of high sastrugi, and that morning I felt quite worn out when I harnessed myself to the sled. It was difficult to get any warmth in my body, even though I was moving as fast as I possibly could.

It was overcast, and even though the wind had dropped a little, it was still blowing quite hard. To find some protection, I tightened the drawstring of my anorak hood. After a while, it was clear that I had tightened it too much, and my facemask was starting to ice up. Unthinkingly, I scraped off the ice with my bare nails. The second time I took off my mittens to do some more scraping, my fingertips were white. I flapped my arms, trying to restore the circulation in my fingertips, but without success. I still couldn't get any warmth into my body, even though I continued to move with all my might. I didn't even stop to eat; I simply went on and on like a maniac, but the cold wouldn't release its grip. I shivered and froze, my fingers were beginning to hurt, and I gave up for the day at about 1:00 p.m.

For the first time on the journey, I let the Primus burn for half an hour to warm the tent. My fingers were hurting terribly, I was shivering and freezing in my sleeping bag, and I even put on my fleece trousers, which until now I hadn't used. During the evening, the weather lifted, and eventually the temperature inside the tent became quite pleasant.

The freezing trials of that day had been one way of commemorating Amundsen and his men, and now I celebrated with hot chocolate and a piece of cake. As I lay reading in my sleeping bag to keep warm, I suddenly heard the drone of a motor. It sounded like a snowmobile. I looked out of the tent but saw nothing. Finally, I caught sight of ANI's little orange Cessna flying low overhead. It came from the direction of the South Pole and circled round me, flapping its wings. I waved back with my anorak. That tiny glimpse of civilization was the only one I would have for fifty days.

"SILENT NIGHT, HOLY NIGHT"

As I approached the South Pole, the sastrugi were diminishing in size, and during the last week I was actually able to remove the skins from my skis. It was wonderful to move without them, even if it's an exaggeration to say that my skis were gliding. With skins, I had to force the skis forward or lift them at every step; at least now I needed less strength to do so.

I was now quite certain of arriving on Christmas Eve, and my thoughts flew to those at home, to Christmas, and to Christmas songs, which mean so much to us in Norway and are distinct from hymns. One particular song went round and round in my head—as much of it as I could remember, that is—and I was unable to concentrate on anything else. I was annoyed at being unable to remember all the verses.

In the wee hours of December 19, I woke up feeling that something was awry. It was silent, exactly as if I had been wearing earplugs. I nearly had a kind of doomsday feeling; strange thoughts of war and atom bombs raced through my head. I hadn't thought much about the world beyond my narrow confines all this time, and now the conflicts in Eastern Europe occurred to me. It was astonishing to observe how quickly I was torn out of one state of mind and plunged into another.

Carefully, and a little anxiously, I opened the tent zipper and looked out. It was dead calm, with an unbelievable, deafening silence. It was my first day in the Antarctic without wind. For the first time I had a feeling of being completely alone. The wind had been enervating, but I had grown used to it, and it had become a traveling companion.

The wind could vary in the course of the day. In general, a gale or stiff breeze had blown every day. For some hours, it might drop to a light breeze, which seemed almost like complete calm. On the first few days, the roar of the wind got on my nerves. One can get used to most things, but I was worn out by the noise. During the first half of the journey, the wind blew from the right; at the halfway point, it was dead against me for three days, before it veered and came from the left.

I opened the tent door and sat for a long time in my sleeping bag, staring out at a serene white expanse and a blue sky. Huge snow crystals were glittering in the sun. I crawled back into the sleeping bag and felt happy, rested, and satisfied. I was exactly five days away from the South Pole.

The last few days were like a fairy tale. The wind had almost completely vanished. The silence seemed overwhelming, almost oppressive. There were few sastrugi, and I was moving over a gleaming white carpet lined with huge snowflakes. I once stopped next to one that was as big as a walnut, glistening brightly, and had the insane idea that someone must have lost a diamond. I knew how brittle it really was and giggled at the episode for hours.

On the day before Christmas Eve, the South Pole base came into sight like a mirage on the horizon. I removed my compass mounting and began steering toward the base. The struggles with high sastrugi, the cold, wind, and crevasses were all forgotten. Since everything had gone so well, I actually began thinking about where my next expedition might take me.

I had imagined that this would be *the* expedition of my life and that after it was finished perhaps I would rest content. As it turns out, that didn't seem to be the case. I thought of climbing Mount Vinson on the way home or perhaps Aconcagua. Obviously, I hadn't lost my taste for adventure.

That day, I thought a great deal of those at home. Previously, I had deliberately not thought of them too often, having decided to banish any longing for home. It would have been wasted energy, seeing that I had spent so many years longing to be here. I thought of Birgitte, tearing around the shops at home to buy Christmas presents at the last minute, as was her habit. She would undoubtedly remember everyone this year as well. I could almost smell the dried mutton ribs and sauerkraut of the traditional Christmas dinner that we usually prepared around this time. For the first time on the whole expedition, I felt hungry.

After three hours, the three small dots on the horizon disappeared, and I had to put on the compass mounting again. Each day so far, making camp had been automatic. That evening I savored every little action; it was all so melancholy. After the dots at the South Pole had come into view, I felt that the journey had gone far too quickly. I had postponed photography and video recording and recognized that if they were to be done at all it would have to be now.

But my frostbitten fingertips were hurting. They had turned blue and quickly became sore if I didn't keep them warm, so I procrastinated yet again. I fell asleep under a brightly shining sun at 89°50′12″ south latitude.

GOURMET LUNCH AND CHAMPAGNE

At eleven o'clock the next morning, the three black dots appeared on the horizon once more, the same three dots that had seemed a mirage the previous morning, when I stood on a rise, but had subsequently vanished. The terrain here was also undulating, but not so markedly as before. From photographs and what I had read, I knew that the biggest dot was the "dome," a hemispherical structure erected over a number of buildings.

"Great God! This is an awful place," wrote Scott in his diary when he reached the South Pole. The closer I approached the base, the more I agreed with him, even though our opinions were based on completely different premises. It was not beautiful there. I thought of the hopeful mood of Scott's party when they approached the South Pole eighty-three years ago and how inexpressibly crushed they were when they saw Amundsen's tent. There was no disappointment in store for me. The worst that could happen was that I wouldn't be allowed to set foot on the base. I was exceedingly curious about what was going on there, considering that the Americans were so intent on keeping the base open.

I thought about the "old boys" who had helped me. Thanks to their sufferings, which I had read about so often, I was prepared to freeze far more than I did. Admittedly, one entry in my diary reads:

Liv, if you begin thinking about another expedition to the Arctic or Antarctic, don't forget how horribly cold it was, how it cut through to the marrow, when you broke camp this morning. You had to move for all you were worth for 45 minutes in order to get some warmth back into your body!

I tried to remember the freezing cold, but it's incredible how quickly one suppresses what is unpleasant. Now that it wasn't blowing, the temperature seemed comfortable, even at −32 degrees Celsius (−26 degrees Fahrenheit). Only my two blue fingers were freezing.

I was moving with my gaze fixed on the South Pole base when I suddenly saw a light dancing toward me. I took some time to realize that it was a snowmobile. It was carrying two members of the Japanese expedition on their way back to the Thiel Mountains to retrieve gasoline canisters. We exchanged congratulations. They had reached the base a couple of days before me and were absolutely beaming with delight over their journey.

As I came closer to the base, I saw the ceremonial South Pole with its line of national flags standing nearest the dome and then, some way off, the geographical South Pole with its sign and pedestal. I saw people moving, and after a little while recognized the Japanese film crew that had accompanied Susumu Nakamura. They were filming my last few meters to the Pole. I stood bent over my ski poles, tears filling my mask, and tried to regain control of myself. Many emotions raced through me; there was a kind of vacuum in my head. The Japanese were sensitive; they saw that I was crying, and they wanted to withdraw, but I persuaded them to stay to take the necessary pictures, and they clicked away with determination.

After a little while, someone named Bob Farrell arrived. He was on the night shift in the cargo department, and for a few nights he had been looking out for me. He said he was glad to have

I am wiping away tears and can finally release my joy. The stake in front of me marks the geographical South Pole.

"found" me; the base had been expecting me for the past day or two. He was kind and forthcoming and made me feel welcome. I unharnessed myself from the sled and went into the dome with him. At the entrance to the canteen stood a really gaudy American Christmas tree with tinsel, decorations, and flashing fairy lights. The first person I met nodded casually and asked if a plane had arrived. ANI runs a few flights every year from Patriot Hills to the South Pole, and eventually I realized that those passengers, rich tourists on a quick visit, were not looked upon with favor at the base.

The ceiling of the canteen was the usual height, but I felt extra tall, at least three meters (ten feet), and bowed my head as I entered. It felt as if the ceiling were coming down toward me.

The warmth hit me like a brick wall. I wafted in—the first time in fifty days that I had moved so far without rucksack and sled. The people working in the kitchen recognized me and looked as if they had seen a ghost. Some of them congratulated and embraced me with tears in their eyes. Once again, I too was somewhat moved. Subsequently, they said that I looked incredibly healthy, as if I had been on a day excursion. They had expected to see a worn-out wreck with a face covered in frostbite.

I was given a cup of coffee and was introduced to Eric Chiang, head of the American Antarctic program at the National Science Foundation. We arranged to meet the station manager and the station scientific leader after I had had a shower. People crowded out to congratulate me. Some of them accompanied me to the shower, where I was given towels and clean clothes.

It was an indescribable relief to remove underclothes that hadn't been changed for fifty days, and the shower was heavenly. I observed that I had lost the ten kilos I'd put on before starting. I let the water run on and on until suddenly it stopped. Afterward, I was informed that those at the base were allowed exactly two minutes in the shower, twice a week. So far south, it costs several dollars to melt enough snow for a liter of water. I dared not think what my shower must have cost, but I was forgiven.

My meeting with the station manager, JP (John Parlen), and the station scientific leader, Jane Dionne, was heartfelt and friendly. They had previously felt somewhat embarrassed at how they had been compelled to treat those who arrived at the South Pole under their own steam. After all, there aren't very many of us. People like me were previously given clandestine help by the staff of the base while the official attitude was extremely hostile. Now a change of policy was in progress, and this year's expeditions were guinea pigs. While we were at the base, politicians from Washington, D.C., were to pay an official visit. At the time, plans were in place to build another base at the South Pole, for which official appropriations are required.

I was given permission to move about freely and visit all the research installations, provided only that I followed the rules in force, and I was allowed one meal a day. I expressed my gratitude for the hospitality and explained that, since my flight would not arrive before January 6, I would like to reciprocate by doing something useful. This offer was well received, and since much of the work in the kitchen depended on volunteers, that's where I was placed. As a scullion, I could have all the meals I might want. The only limitation as a guest was that the base had no extra living space, which meant I had to sleep in my own tent. I didn't feel particularly tempted to sleep indoors in the heat, so I would have stayed in my tent in any case.

About an hour after my arrival, I found myself in the midst of a fantastic Christmas brunch. I was quite overwhelmed by all the people, all the different impressions, and the warm welcome. When someone came up to me and said that he had seen me before, I thought for a moment that he was trying to chat me up. *Oh, no, not that corny line,* I thought, answering rather stiffly, not to say discouragingly. Where on earth could I have met this American before? He refused to give up and asked if I had ever been in Park City, Utah. In fact, I had been there, as a ski instructor in 1978. "Sure!" he said, brightening up. "You taught me cross-country skiing!" Really and truly, it's a small world.

They lacked nothing at the South Pole. All kinds of fresh fruit were on the table—grapes, strawberries, kiwifruit, bananas, pineapples—and cakes and champagne, as much as we wanted.

Since it was Christmas Eve in Norway, I was allowed to call home, a unique privilege, even allowing for the fact that the charges had to be reversed. It was the middle of the night, and at home a sleepy daughter lifted the receiver. Linn was astonished to hear the voice of an American telephone operator asking if she would accept a collect call from me in the United States. She didn't consider that the base at the South Pole was American. "Liv, where are you?" she demanded.

"I'm in New York, having a party," I said, and felt it wasn't far from the truth.

"In New York!" Linn screeched. "You must be crazy—everyone thinks you're at the South Pole!"

With modern communication and rapid transport, it was easy to get confused. Einar was celebrating at the next-door neighbor's house. From the transmittal they had received on my position, they knew that I had arrived at my destination. That's how I learned that the Argos had worked after all. It was a relief.

The next day, I made contact with Einar, and we had a long talk. We were as far apart as it was possible to be on this earth, yet we felt so close. The line was absolutely clear, just as if I were calling from next door. Now I allowed myself to long for him; I wished he were there and could share it all with me. My family had received messages regularly and had understood several weeks earlier that I was planning to have the South Pole as a Christmas present. He was surprised that I'd met so many crevasses but was glad not to have known about them at the time.

The base had been established during the International Geophysical Year (IGY) of 1957–58. The American scientist Dr. Lloyd Berkner (after whom Berkner Island is named) suggested the date because it was expected to coincide with particularly strong solar radiation.

At the same time, the Soviet Union had established the most inaccessible Antarctic base, at the farthest point from the coast. Many other scientific bases were established at various points along the continental coast. One outcome of the IGY was the

Antarctic Treaty, with the original twelve participating countries as signatories: the United States, the Soviet Union, Argentina, Australia, Belgium, Chile, France, Great Britain, Japan, New Zealand, Norway, and South Africa. Among other things, the treaty made Antarctica a demilitarized zone.

Coincidentally, during the IGY (not part of it, but far better known among the general public), the first crossing of Antarctica took place by the English explorer Sir Vivian Fuchs. He completed what Sir Ernest Shackleton had tried and failed to do in 1914–16. Fuchs started from the Filchner Ice Shelf, northeast of Berkner Island, at a base named after Shackleton. Using snow tractors, Fuchs crossed the continent to the Scott Base at McMurdo Sound via the South Pole, meeting great difficulties with crevasses along the way.

Meanwhile, Sir Edmund Hillary, the New Zealander who first conquered Mount Everest, had traveled in the opposite direction to lay depots; finding easier terrain and hence making quicker time, he made an unscheduled excursion to the South Pole, anticipating Fuchs. Hillary thus became the first since Scott to reach the South Pole overland. The very first by any means was the commander of Operation Deep Freeze, Admiral George Dufek, commemorated in the map of Antarctica by the Dufek Massif in the Pensacola Mountains. He was flown in from the McMurdo Base on October 31, 1956, and planted the Stars and Stripes at the South Pole for the first time.

The original South Pole base was built in 1957; since then, it has been buried ten meters under the snow and moved about a kilometer from the Pole. The blue aluminum dome, which is now the dominating structure at the South Pole and the center of the present base, was built between 1971 and 1975. The dome covers buildings with offices, a dining hall, a gymnasium, workshops, garages, and accommodations for the staff of about thirty who spend the winter there. The old base is now buried under so much snow that the ceilings are in danger of collapse, and entry is forbidden. Access is maintained by a shaft that is always kept open, and a year or two ago, when the juicing machine at the new base broke down, it was simply replaced by hoisting up the one abandoned at the old base. Almost everything is available at the South Pole; it's almost bizarre, considering how far it is to the nearest supermarket. Soon after I arrived, I was asked if I wanted anything in particular, and after half an hour, a magnificent home-made pizza appeared, with huge olives, red wine, and an avocado!

During my time at the base in 1994, I discovered it had a comprehensive library and many long shelves stacked with new and old movies on video. The staff could keep in touch with their nearest and dearest at home by email: they send their messages and might have a reply within twenty minutes. They could phone anywhere in the world by satellite when it's over the Southern Hemisphere, and in 1996 there was talk of receiving live television transmissions. Veterans at the base were saying that if that happened, things would never be the same again. The only things I didn't find, and which I had expected at an American base, were big burgers and Coca-Cola!

After three days with 130 enthusiastic Americans, Eric Clapton and the Eagles at full blast, in 80 degrees Fahrenheit, I was more worn out than at any time underway on my expedition. I escaped into my tent and lay staring for several hours.

Even there it wasn't absolutely quiet. As many as four Hercules aircraft from McMurdo Sound landed at the South Pole every day, and bulldozers rumbled and creaked as they passed my tent. For the first week it was difficult to sleep. Presumably, it was the abrupt change from hard work and a strictly disciplined existence to light kitchen work and the numerous sounds that robbed me of my sleep.

The puffiness in my face caused by the cold subsided and left me looking somewhat ravaged. I was wrinkled and a trifle drawn, and I actually resembled my great-grandmother at the age of eighty. The fifty days I had spent alone on the expedition disappeared in all the fuss. The days of calm I had looked forward to, with time to absorb my experience, somehow never materialized.

It was a relief when Cato, Lars, and Odd Harald, of the Unarmed Expedition, finally arrived and all the attention could be divided among four people. They got the same sincere reception, together with jobs in the cargo division. There were tons of extra food and equipment, and the base had decided to ship some of it back to McMurdo Sound during the course of the season. On one of the first evenings after the guys had arrived, we sat down together over a few bottles of wine and talked about our respective journeys. We didn't need much wine to get even happier than we already were, and the whole base soon became aware of our little party. The fact that we managed to return to our tents safely and turn up at work the next morning consolidated our reputations as Vikings.

Such outposts attract a special kind of person, and, as I've noticed on Svalbard, under such circumstances people are more intimate. At the South Pole, I had many long and enjoyable conversations and made several new friends. The atmosphere at the base was wonderful: friendly, encouraging, outgoing, and informal. The staff came from a great variety of backgrounds. They ranged from a Nobel Prize–winning astrophysicist, Bob Wilson (of the Big Bang), to artists, ski bums, guides, cooks, teachers, and aging hippies.

I felt most attuned to the women in the kitchen. Lizan, the washing-up "boss," wrote songs and played the guitar in her spare time and was wondering if she'd found Mr. Right (who also happened to be working at the base). Darby was a fifty-year-old housewife, artistically gifted, who found herself in a vacuum after her husband had left her. She produced some drawings for the New Year's party; they were the first she had done in a year. Perhaps she was beginning to recover and could start looking life in the face again. Nancy had the same scullion job as Darby. Nancy was an artist, liked cooking, and could bake really good bread. She, too, came from Park City, and it turned out that we had common acquaintances there.

Bill was one of the kitchen volunteers. He was an instructor, teaching the scientists how to cope with conditions in the field. He led the rescue operation during Monica Kristensen's Aurora expedition the year before. Ann was a freelance photographer and disliked kitchen work as heartily as I did. She was strongly attracted by the Antarctic and had been there on several occasions. Kristine, one of the cooks, came from the Seattle area and was bubbling with laughter and smiles. She was divorced but not quite finished with her husband. The doctor at the South Pole, Eileen Sverdrup, was descended from H. U. Sverdrup, a Norwegian scientist who was with Amundsen on his navigation of the Northeast Passage in the *Maud* in 1918–20. She and many others at the base were fascinated by polar history, and we spent many hours telling each other anecdotes about the "old guys." P.J. was a scientist and had brought his mountain bike to ride between the various buildings. Erik had dreadlocks and a delightful attitude toward life. On New Year's Eve, he hoisted a new flag among the others, with the motto SO FAR—SO WHAT. Something to ponder.

Emily was the only cook who was going to stay the winter. She was also the vocalist in the group called the Pole Cats, but she was best at preparing food. Don had Swedish blood and was a sight for sore eyes. He was a mountain guide at home in Oregon. Glen, his girlfriend, was an artist, a firefighter, and a former member of the U.S. alpine ski team. Spore was from Wyoming. He was deeply interested in my equipment and dreamed of crossing

Greenland one day. I didn't meet one C3 type (someone living an everyday nine-to-five life) at the South Pole.

Some manage to live for the rest of the year on what they save up here at 90° south. They don't earn particularly high salaries, nor do they pay lower taxes than at home. But they have free room and board, and there isn't much to spend their pay on, apart from wine and spirits, which are rationed and cheap. Those involved in running the base work multiple shifts. The scientists work virtually around the clock as well. The summer months must be exploited to the utmost.

When I wasn't on kitchen duty, I was either in the library or in the canteen. I had the opportunity to learn about some of the research projects and accompany the bulldozer drivers responsible for maintaining the water supply. They fetched snow in huge boxes from an area well away from the landing strip and emptied it into a tank that always had to be filled to a certain level. This was the source of drinking water. The snow was melted by a gas burner.

It was hugely interesting to see the various research posts around the base. They give us greater insight into our ecosystems and show how important it is to protect the natural environment. I was particularly interested in the Clean Air Project, after all the press coverage at home in Norway in connection with the Aurora expeditions. The Norwegian press somehow gave me the impression that the project was shrouded in secrecy. It was conducted in a special zone around the Pole. Had the Americans been doing something mysterious there? We explained our doubts to them, but they replied that they were hiding nothing. We were free to go into the zone with a Geiger counter to investigate, but we had to say so in advance. The sensors that have been put in the zone are extraordinarily sensitive, so much so, in fact, that during violent winter storms they have actually recorded salt all the way from the sea, more than 1,400 kilometers (875 miles) away! We were told that the harsh American reaction after the Norwegian Aurora expeditions descended on the base was due to their having taxied into the Clean Air Sector with a Twin Otter without requesting permission or reporting their intention. Many valuable observations were destroyed.

Christmas celebrations were scarcely over before everyone at the base had started preparations for another party. New Year's Eve was going to be something special. The last few days before I arrived, I had wondered idly how the occasion would be celebrated at the South Pole. Einar and I had spent the previous New Year's Eve on the top of Kolsås, a low mountain to the west of Oslo. It was a fantastic Norwegian winter night, lit by hundreds of fireworks. We skied home, using Telemark turns, in moonlight and perfect snow.

The Pole Cats were rehearsing during every spare moment, and the cooks were preparing a huge buffet. We decorated the canteen with green parachutes that had been used to drop supplies to scientists spread out over Antarctica. People decked themselves out in everything from togas to dinner jackets. Outside, in a dead calm, a brilliant midnight sun was shining, and some of us sat against a wall sunning ourselves—at −25 degrees Celsius (−13 degrees Fahrenheit) in the shade.

The evening dissolved into a wild party, the likes of which I'd rarely seen. At a late hour, someone raided the store of shaving cream and squirted it over the revelers. It was lovely to smell shaving cream again—and I had an acute attack of longing for Einar. At midnight, a few of us went over to the post marking the geographical South Pole. It was a little odd to think that the globe was rotating around this "axis." The International Date Line was here, so we held hands and ran around shouting, "1994, 1995, 1994, 1995 . . ."

Happy! On my way back to civilization. Photograph by Knut Bry.

The South Pole was an interesting place to be, but once it was 1995 all around the world, I wanted to go home. After the New Year's festivities, there was something of a void, and my thoughts turned more and more often to those at home. After the telephone conversations on Christmas Eve and Christmas Day, I hadn't had any contact with the outside world.

The weather was brilliant, and nothing suggested that we wouldn't be picked up as planned. We received confirmation that our flight would arrive on January 6, and on the evening before, we Norwegians hosted a farewell dinner. We served Norwegian fish soup and baked salmon to all 140 people at the base. Afterward, there was a spontaneous party.

The Twin Otter from ANI landed the next morning. Three men connected with Cato's Unarmed Expedition were in the plane. Knut Bry had returned as the expedition photographer, and they had a cold and busy day. More than a hundred corporate logos had to be photographed at the Pole. It all took time. The rest of us simply waited and waited. Deciding on another farewell party, some women fetched a bottle. The hours passed quickly, and people shared many cheerful anecdotes, which made the departure easier. It's sad to part with new friends.

We flew back to Patriot Hills in brilliant weather, following almost exactly the route along which I had come. I saw the undulating landscape, so blue and white and wonderful, and the crevassed ridges. I tried to remember what the days had been like down there on the ice, but they had already receded far into the past.

BACK TO CIVILIZATION

We landed at Patriot Hills around breakfast time, Chilean time. One of the sponsors of the Unarmed Expedition provided lobsters and champagne that had been flown in from the mainland. After the fantastic flight and the warm reception with a somewhat unusual breakfast, our mood rose sky-high.

Everyone was eager to be allowed time on the satellite telephone to talk to their loved ones. I was able to talk to Einar and the girls, to my parents, and to Wanda on her mobile phone in the Norwegian mountains. It's incredible what these satellites can manage. Various journalists called us from Norway; most were naturally most interested in talking to Cato, who with the Unarmed Expedition had accomplished something amazing.

The two frostbitten fingers on my right hand were still blue and sore. The doctor at the South Pole thought I would lose the tip of my thumb, but I believed it would be all right. I've seen worse frostbite that ended well, but this looked ugly. My kitchen job of washing dishes fit splendidly with the treatment; movement and warm water improved the circulation.

At Patriot Hills there was a Spanish military surgeon who specialized in cold injuries. He quickly began treating me. I was given pills to thin my blood and others to dilate the blood vessels. Twice a day I moved my fingers in a warm iodine solution to prevent infection in my thumb, which had an open wound, and the circulation in my fingers was stimulated by an electric current twice daily. After the first treatment, my thumb felt better immediately. I followed the treatment the entire time I was at Patriot Hills and was given strict instructions to continue the regime at home. I was also advised to drink a glass or two of red wine every day to help renew my blood supply. I'm a little afraid of pills, so on returning home I chose the wine treatment, while trying to keep my fingers warm and moving them. Otherwise, I spent the three days at Patriot Hills skiing in the area; it was wonderful to see mountains and rocks again after the everlasting snow and ice. We also adjusted to Chilean time.

I had looked forward to perhaps meeting Einar in Santiago and then spending a few days on Easter Island. At home they had other ideas. NRK wanted me to return in time for a new TV talk show on January 14. That meant the journey home had to proceed exactly as planned. But many a traveler has been weather-bound for weeks at Patriot Hills.

For fun, we decided to try to hitchhike from Antarctica, weather permitting. Lars, of the Unarmed Expedition, had to sacrifice his jacket in order to make the right contacts. It so happened that the Chilean Air Force was planning its first flight to Patriot Hills since a crash landing there during the 1980s. Their intention was simply to touch down, unload some fuel drums, and take off again. We wanted to be on that plane. We pursued our inquiries through several channels, and eventually our request was granted.

On January 10, we settled into the military version of a Hercules aircraft, a decided downgrade from the amenities to which we had become accustomed. We missed Holly from ANI and a little luxury, but we disposed ourselves to sleep on the floor, on our sleds, or in the netting seats. After seven hours, we landed at Punta Arenas, shaken in every bone.

The landing of the first Chilean Air Force Antarctic flight in a decade attracted considerable attention, and Cato advanced toward the waiting TV cameras as if to the manor born. Officers, politicians, and other notables seemed rather confused by the sight of the peculiar, colorful group slouching out of the fuselage with strange equipment. We were hardly a well-drilled military squad in uniform. Anne from ANI walked over from the other end of the airfield. She could hardly believe the reports from Betty that we had hitched a ride with the Chilean Air Force and shook her head, telling us how mad we Norwegians were.

The first few hours after landing, the smells were overpowering. The odor of warm asphalt and aviation fuel was splendid. The scent of all the flowers, mixed with sea air, on the way to Punta Arenas was lovely. We checked into the Hotel Condor Plata again, followed by hectic faxing to sponsors, the press, employers, and family and friends at home.

After two days, I flew to Santiago. Norwegian Ambassador Reiulf Steen met me at the airport, together with Joar Hoel Larsen, NRK's reporter in Latin America. I took the opportunity to thank the ambassador for his help with my sled on the way down. NRK wanted my equipment back home in time for their talk show. The ambassador intervened once more when difficulties threatened. With his help, everything was arranged within thirty minutes, and we had time for coffee and a chat before departure. Steen was relieved that this year's Norwegian expeditions to the South Pole had gone so well. Both had enjoyed highly favorable press in Argentina and Chile. Another Norwegian Antarctic expedition, which shall remain nameless, had previously departed without paying its bills, which had brought much unpleasantness to the ambassadors in both countries, so Steen was unrestrainedly delighted over the impression left by the Norwegians on this occasion.

There's always a sense of anticipation when sitting in an aircraft seat. Now and then there are odd encounters with passengers who share your interests. At Buenos Aires, an Englishman sat next to me. He worked in computers and had been on a business trip; I explained that I had been in the Antarctic. He talked about his twelve-year-old son, who was writing a school essay about Scott of the Antarctic, and then started in on a long dissertation on his—and his son's—Antarctic hero. I ventured a few critical remarks, and after a while he asked what I had been doing in Antarctica and why I seemed so well informed. I explained that I had skied to the South Pole and that I was on my way home to Norway. He nearly choked on his red wine and looked at me in sheer disbelief. The schoolmasterly manner disappeared and the stiff upper lip loosened somewhat. In England he had heard of my expedition.

Wanda was worried that I'd be unable to sleep during the long flight home, because she knew all about the hectic schedule awaiting me. I would have exactly one hour at home after arriving in Oslo before I had to be at the TV studios. She had sent me two sleeping pills via the little Norwegian delegation that came to receive the Unarmed Expedition at the South Pole—two in case I lost one, she had instructed, but I hadn't read her accompanying letter carefully enough beforehand.

After a sumptuous dinner in the air, I decided that sleep would be in order, and I took both pills. I rarely take pills, and an aspirin alone knocks me out. I didn't wake up until we were in Amsterdam, the Englishman in the next seat impressed by my ability to relax. At the airport in Amsterdam I was reunited with the man in my life. Einar had flown there that morning to meet me. It was lovely to see him again and wonderful to have the opportunity to talk together alone and undisturbed before all the fuss at home.

The arrival hall in the Oslo airport was a frenzy of family and friends, fellow club members, journalists, sponsors, banners, and cheering. It took a long time before I caught sight of my nearest and dearest. I was deeply moved and noticed that many others were as well. I was especially glad to be reunited with my mother and father. Mother was crying, and I felt a stab of conscience. They must have been more worried than I was prepared to admit, or that they were willing to reveal, before I left. Certainly they hadn't enjoyed themselves nearly as much as I had all these weeks.

The first questions fired at me by the journalists concerned my frostbitten fingers, and they seemed almost a little disappointed to hear that no amputation was likely.

I drove home, took a quick shower, and changed. We arrived too late for the TV rehearsal, and there was a noticeably strained atmosphere in the studio. I was somewhat disconcerted. The journey I was supposed to talk about had been completed nearly a month earlier, and the memories were somewhat distant. The presenter didn't seem particularly well prepared; he barely listened to my answers and instead moved his finger down a sheet of paper to the next question. After two days of continuous travel, I wasn't exactly the easiest subject to interview. When a weekly magazine announced that it was giving us a free trip to Hawaii, my immediate reaction was, "Do I have to? It'll be hot!"—before Einar managed to instill some enthusiasm into me. My first vacation together with Einar and the girls had been on Mallorca, and it wasn't pure unadulterated pleasure for all of us. They constantly remind me that I sat in the shade, reading, for two weeks. I could see them snickering at the thought of another seaside vacation.

After the TV program, we went straight to a restaurant, where friends and sponsors had arranged a welcome home party. I came to life again, and we didn't get home until four o'clock in the morning. The following day, I had an appointment with journalists for a ski tour in my old haunts outside Oslo. Even though I was horribly tired and my sense of balance was still poor, it was lovely to be on light skis with light equipment again. I felt quite naked without all the heavy gear.

With interviews in newspapers, in journals, and on the radio, the following weeks seemed to melt into one. Most inquiries came from abroad. There was particular interest in Germany, where I took part in talk shows. I found it hard to settle down, even though I went skiing in Nordmarka as often as I could. At the South Pole, I had looked forward to being together with my family, reading, and taking long ski tours. Einar was engrossed in writing his dissertation, something he ought to have done while I was on my journey, but he couldn't concentrate then. Now he had to make up for lost time.

Wanda and I went to Berlin to appear on a TV show. We spent our free time in the hotel room analyzing what I really wanted to make of my expedition. She made me aware of the fact that memories are short; I must either marshal my thoughts right away or give up. Before we left Berlin, I had decided to give at least one lecture.

I tried to gather my thoughts and began to work on the text and pictures for my lecture. Now I paid for my laziness with camera and video while I was in the field. I didn't have many photographs or video clips illustrating what the journey had been like. The sponsors in Italy were not exactly pleased. Luckily, two cameramen came to Norway and filmed dramatic scenes in a whiteout—at Norefjell, a mountain almost in my backyard.

I was still a little disoriented, and the woman in the photographs and the video seemed somehow not me. It was difficult to recapture the pleasant atmosphere, the peace, and the state of mind I felt while on my expedition.

SO FAR—SO WHAT: Erik's flag at the South Pole popped up constantly in my thoughts.

WHAT NEXT?

How strange—always sadness at parting.
Now it is as if one nonetheless cannot tear
oneself away from this forlorn desolation of
ice, glaciers, cold and drudgery.

—Fridtjof Nansen, 1912

Before departure, I had signed a contract for a book about the expedition. Now, after all the fuss, I was no longer sure of myself. By nature, I'm somewhat shy, so to be the center of attention doesn't really suit me. Besides, plenty of books about demanding expeditions had recently appeared. Wanda knew very well what was on my mind and left me in no doubt of her opinion: "Coward! Typical female! Lots of girls are waiting for your story—they need it! Don't let them down!"

As my press agent, Wanda had observed that there was greater interest in the men's expedition than in mine. While I was away, she experienced on my behalf the attitude of the press and the sponsors I had met before departing: it was an eye-opener for her. She had worked among the press for many years and knew that it was hidebound, but until now she had never understood to what degree.

I'd had a desire to articulate the experiences and emotions that preceded the expedition, besides the events and thoughts while I was in the snows, but now I almost recoiled from the thought of doing so. These are the chapters I often miss when men write about their expeditions. Perhaps they are genuinely more concerned with practical matters, or perhaps they have been trained not to look inward.

It's generally understood that skiing to the South Pole with a sled weighing a hundred kilos (220 pounds) behind you is a harsh trial. Naturally, I could have dredged up all the words that evoke freezing cold, sweat, and struggle and gone on and on in a blow-by-blow chronicle of every single day. But I felt that the real story lay elsewhere, that it began long before my first steps on the Antarctic continent. It was just as demanding and much more difficult to express in words.

The last six months before departure had been hectic. I had spent every minute of each day on work and training, and many weeks passed by on the expedition before I felt at one with nature, before the great white snowfields gripped me, before I found peace and began breathing differently. The calm I felt when I reached the South Pole vanished there and has since been difficult to recapture. Now and then, while I was underway, I looked forward to sitting in front of the fire with a good book, even to doing work around the house.

And still the books I hadn't yet managed to read in the year following my trip remained unopened on the bookshelves, nor had I managed to unwind and find myself, even by skiing and cycling, as I used to do. I brooded and felt thoroughly restless. Ought I to return to work before my leave of absence expired? I broke out into a sweat at the mere thought of a regular day at the office and imagined that never again could I cope with an ordinary, settled, everyday job.

Everybody asked about my next expedition and assumed that it would be to the North Pole. I had never dreamed about skiing there, but I had many other dreams and desires, which came crowding in one after the other. I wanted to travel, and there's much I wanted to learn.

Perhaps I hadn't divested myself of a dream but rather had become the victim of even more longing desires. If I chose to arrange my life in this direction, I'd be able to take part in stimulating projects for many years to come. Others were now seeing me as a potential partner or expedition member. I now knew that I can push my own limits further and withstand most strains. How restless could I allow myself to be?

———————————

I feel immensely privileged to have had the opportunity of completing this expedition to the South Pole. It will forever remain the great journey of my life. My entire being is full of memories I can retrieve and enjoy for the rest of my life, even when workaday existence returns.

It would give me great satisfaction if my expedition to the South Pole in some way helped or inspired others to find the key to themselves so that they might realize the talents and abilities they possess. I would like everyone to experience the same bubbling happiness I feel within myself after having achieved my great adventure.

EPILOGUE

On Christmas Eve 2019, twenty-five years had passed since I arrived at the South Pole. And when this English edition of my book is published, it will have been twenty-five years since I wrote this book. Those twenty-five years have also been an adventure—and as in all adventures there have been ups and downs. I attempted to climb Mount Everest from Tibet in 1996 but got altitude sickness at 7,000 meters and fortunately descended safely. Ten years ago Einar and I divorced, but the years have given me six grandchildren. I still travel the world lecturing and am a guide in the Arctic and Antarctic.

When I was at the South Pole in 1994, my plan had been to return to work as a high school teacher in literature and sports, but that did not happen. I was asked to give lectures around the world and as a result never returned to the classroom. I did become a student, however, after being inspired during my preparations for a guest lecture I gave at the Oslo Business School under the theme "risk management." I saw then that everything that happens in an expedition also happens in all organizations, from a small family to a large group. What is the vision? What is the goal? Who should we have on the team? How should we communicate? What is the risk? How do we choose with whom to work or live? Scott chose his men based on status and appearance. Amundsen chose his men based on the knowledge and personal qualities he needed from his participants for his expedition. Scott and his men died.

When Nansen and Hjalmar Johansen, a loyal team member with experience from the Arctic whom Nansen chose to join him on this ambitious expedition, left the *Fram* to reach the North Pole, the entire crew was relieved. Nansen was frustrated that the operation hadn't gone as planned—the researchers he had wanted on the expedition didn't come, and he took out his frustration with unfriendly comments toward the crew. Shackleton is my favorite when it comes to communicating with his men: he's often considered the world's best expedition leader even though he did not achieve any of the great goals he had set. How he treated his men and maintained their motivation in extreme and dramatic situations has made him a mythical role model of leadership. And on and on.

I earned a master's degree in management and since then have combined practice and theory by delivering leadership courses and lectures. Education has always been and remains my driving force. On my way to the South Pole, I thought of students who had no idea what they were going to become or spend their lives doing, and I started writing a book for young people about how they could achieve their dreams. After a couple of years, I received a letter from Ann Bancroft wondering if I could imagine joining her on an expedition across the Antarctic continent; we could use this expedition to support education about Antarctica and help young people achieve their dreams. I still remember the letter and my reaction. Was it possible that a woman was thinking along the same lines as I was on the other side of the Atlantic Ocean?

I traveled to Minnesota to meet Ann and the team she had assembled for the project. We went for walks and talked together about everything *except* the expedition across Antarctica. Ann also had a background as a teacher, and on her parents' bookshelves I found polar books that were also on my parents' bookshelves. It was clear from the beginning that we were both passionate about giving young people the tools to create the lives they wanted.

We created two educational programs: Dare to Dream and an interdisciplinary program about Antarctica. We crossed the Antarctic continent in ninety-four days, with six million children in 116 countries following us. During the expedition, we communicated directly to CNN one or two days a week, which gave us 2.1 billion media hits.

When Ann and I saw these numbers after our expedition, we decided to continue working together, combining adventure and education. We have developed a warm friendship, and both of us feel we have found a soul sister in each other. We have undergone several expeditions—most recently, our Access Water project paddling the Ganges River from its source to the sea with a woman from each continent. Our next project is to paddle the Whanganui River in New Zealand, which in 2017 became the first river in the world to gain the same legal rights as a person. And so the work continues.

Eitre, August 2020

ACKNOWLEDGMENTS

Having finished the book, I return my thoughts once more to all of you who helped me on my way with practical, financial, technical, and moral support.

A solo expedition is not a solo project. My heartfelt thanks go first to all of my family, friends, colleagues, and unknown supporters. I also thank Wanda Widerøe. When I found myself unable to afford an overpriced press agent, she volunteered to work without payment. What's more, she got me going with lectures and with this book after my return. She worked unstintingly on editing this book and gave me inspiration, dragging material out of me. We have become fast friends.

Liv Arnesen
Bekkestua, July 20, 1995

Main sponsor: Sector Sport Watches

Other sponsors and supporters (in alphabetical order):

Adventure Network International (ANI) (tour operator in Antarctica; cost the Earth but did the job)

Aftenposten (Oslo newspaper)

Ajungilak (good, warm sleeping bag)

Alfa shoe manufacturers (fantastic ski boots)

Berit and Finn Chr. Arnesen (created me in 1952)

Finn Arnesen AS

Sigmund Arnesen (my brother, who secured many sponsors for me)

Asker og Bærums Budstikke (helpful local newspaper with full-page advertisements)

Åsnes Ski (high-quality skis and mohair skins)

Susan Barr (Norwegian Polar Institute, helped with historical photographs and commented on the historical sections in the book)

Bjørn Basberg (designed the expedition logo)

Paul Bays (designer at Lill-Sport who made my special combined back and sled harness)

Kirsti Behrens (helped with menus, dietary calculations, and food packing)

Bollé (goggles)

Thom Borgen (lawyer who helped me with contracts)

Atle Brunvold (journalist at *Aftenposten,* provided invaluable help with Argos transmissions)

Per Brustad (important man at Sony)

Knut Bry

Ricardo Carcamo (incredibly helpful and encouraging Norwegian vice consul in Punta Arenas)

Bitte Dahl (friend and former teaching colleague who helped greatly with the manuscript)

Devold Stoknes AS (warm, functional woolen underwear)

DHL (gave a small discount on transport of sleds but didn't manage to deliver them on time)

David Durkan (always encouraging supporter with various items of equipment)

Thomas Fearnley's Memorial Fund

Fjellanger Widerøe AS (copying photographs)

Fjellpulken (made a sturdy and light sled)

Pål Erik Foss (a vital Sony guy)

Willy Gautvik (one of the polar veterans with a wealth of knowledge and a glint in his eye)

Grepet ANS

Guriby AS (electrical contractors)

Harald Hammerö (pleasant and helpful marketing manager at Lill-Sport)

Sixten and Maj-Britt Haraldson (encouraging supporters)

Haslum Grafisk AS (postcards)

Jan Erling Haugland (Norwegian Polar Institute; what or whom doesn't he know and where hasn't he been?)

Heien Fotosats AS (helped with prospectus)

Lise and Arnfinn Hejes Fund

Hellanor (excellent burners that I didn't take because unfortunately they couldn't be used in a rarefied atmosphere)

Helsport (tent)

Hesselberg Maskin

Joar Hoel Larsen (opened his home to me in Santiago)

Helge Hoflandsdal (helpful man at Åsnes)

Halvor Holm (helped with my menu and dietary calculations)

Inger Husby (my sister-in-law, who helped to pack food)

Inform Norske Kontormøbler

Interfoto AS (cameras)

Jotun AS (Henning Rørvik, obtained products to mold sleds)

Erling Kagge (the first to go south alone)

Anne Kershaw (director of ANI, provided pleasant cooperation)

Kims AS (potato chips)

KLM (discount on airline tickets)

Arvid Knudsen Transport AS

Gunnar Krogsveen AS

Larsen & Lund—Dekk Partner

Per Erik Lien (my dentist, who gave me a free, thorough checkup and emergency filling material)

Lill-Sport (products)

Nina Lindstad (friend and doctor who equipped first aid kit)

Lube Norsk AS (Piqasol-Q10 pills)

Julie Maske (friend and photographer, helped with final packing in Punta Arenas)

Materialdata AB

Sjur Mørdre (vital supporter)

Ragnar Næss Bygningsartikler AS

Navex (GPS sets)

Nidar Bergene (Stratos with nuts—good, nourishing chocolate)

Tove Nielsen (opened her home in Santiago)

Egil Nilsson (encouraging, helpful man at Interfoto)

No Limits Techware (clothing)

Norkart AS (splendid map for the press and the book)

Norsk Meierier (powdered cream for breakfast)

Norwegian Defense Research Station at Kjeller (Tor Oftedal made my Nansen cooker) and Norwegian Defense battery laboratory at Dal (Mikal Eriksen and his team helped with leads for external lithium batteries for GPS and video camera)

Norwegian Polar Institute (photographs for the book, map of route)

Norwegian Radio Channel 4 (radio channel to receive reports)

Nycomed Jean Mette (Medima gloves and knee and elbow warmers)

Nycomed Pharma (XL-1)

Hallgrim Ødegaard (loaned film for multimedia program)

Jorunn Ore (encouraging and helpful lady at Nycomed Pharma)

Østfold Trykkeri (printing of prospectus)

Børge Ousland (one of the polar boys who really knows his stuff)

Carl Emil Petersen (inspirational supporter, always good humored and encouraging)

Nicolai Prytz, seven years old (my first sponsor, donated 10 kroner—about £1, or $1.45)

Ulf Prytz (understanding boss)

Racal-Tacticom Ltd. (the radio that didn't transmit, but perhaps it was my fault)

Dagfinn Ragg (encouraging and helpful man at Rottefella)

Anders Rasmussen (helpful man at KLM)

Aina Ringerike (energetic supporter)

Johan and Yerina Rock (sponsored me with their savings)

Paul Røer (supporter)

Rottefella (sturdy bindings)

Royal Norwegian Foreign Ministry/Norgesprofil

Ergil Rustadstuen (always served marzipan cake during my visits to the sled factory)

Sætre AS (chocolate biscuits)

Sandvika Veveri

Lonnie Schorer (supporter, translated press reports)

Silva Norge (Antarctic compass)

SINTEF (expertise and freezing chamber)

Skiforeningen (Association for the Promotion of Skiing in Oslo, particularly Knut Almquist, Wanda's understanding supervisor; special thanks to those in charge of the ski tracks for splendid conditions and much pleasure in skiing!)

Sony Norge (lent a Sony Handycam 3CCD video camera)

Stabburet (food during my fattening process, breakfast and lunch during the expedition)

Reiulf Steen (charming and helpful Norwegian ambassador in Chile)

Stibolt-Norge Ski AS (ever-encouraging support of my expeditions, goggles, face masks, and Zig bottles)

Sun Win AS (molded the sleds)

Svalbard Polar Travel AS (encouraging employer)

Charles Swithinbank (proposed the route to the South Pole I finally adopted, along the meridian of 80°30′W)

Swix (ski poles)

Tele-Mobiler (mobile phone services)

Olaf Thommessen (pleasant and helpful man at Stabbur)

Ivar Erik Tollefsen (an expedition leader with hot tips on how
to "sell" myself)

Toro Næringsmiddelindustri (chocolate and black currant
drinks)

Toron AS (in particular Tom Erlandsen, mobile telephones and
pagers)

Arild Vegrim (one of the encouraging polar veterans)

Marianne Weber Nielsen (friend, helped with packing food)

Turi Widerøe (perceptive comments on manuscript)

Wanda Widerøe (press agent, friend, and consultant, also
helped to pack food)

Gjert Wilhelmsen (supporter)

Zürich Assurance (insurance)

METRIC TO STANDARD CONVERSIONS

2½ centimeters = 1 inch
30 centimeters = 1 foot
100 centimeters = 1 meter = 1.1 yards, about 39 inches
1,000 meters = 1 kilometer = 1,100 yards, or five-eighths of a mile
10 kilometers = 6¼ miles
50 kilometers = 31¼ miles
100 kilometers = 62½ miles
1 mile = 1.6 kilometers

1 liter = 1.1 quarts, or 35 ounces by liquid volume
1000 grams = 1 kilogram (or kilo) = 2.2 pounds, or 35 ounces
    by weight
28 grams = 1 ounce
450 grams = 1 pound

degrees Celsius = (degrees Fahrenheit −32) x 5/9

All values are approximate.

EXPEDITION LOG

4 Nov. 94. Transport by snowmobile northward from Patriot Hills and down to the ice at Hercules Inlet. 5 hours by snowmobile. Brilliant sun. Fresh breeze.

STARTING POINT: Hercules Inlet: 79°59′19″S. 79°43′14″W.

(1) 5 Nov. 94. Distance: 10.4 km. Total: 10.4 km. Altitude 420 meters above sea level.

80°02′44″S. 80°09′13″W. Sun. Heavy climbs. Headwind and transverse sastrugi.

(2) 6 Nov. 94. Distance: 11.8 km. Total: 22.2 km. Altitude 720 m.

80°09′13″S. 80°14′16″W. Whiteout, snow, and wind. Difficult hummocks. Stop and camp when I drive ski pole into blue ice.

(3) 7 Nov. 94. Distance: 10.1 km. Total: 32.3 km. Altitude 810 m.

80°14′13″S. 80°28′30″W. Late start due to whiteout. Brilliant afternoon. Wind from right. Many crevasses. Alternate between crampons and skis. Broke through knee-deep once.

(4) 8 Nov. 94. Distance: 19.8 km. Total: 52.1 km. Altitude 810 m.

80°24′00″S. 80°48′20″W. Brilliant day. Breeze. Take it easy and stop around 1700 hours. A little worn out after three hard days. Sit outside in the sun and dry my boots—OUTSIDE.

(5) 9 Nov. 94. Distance: 21.9 km. Total: 74.0 km.

80°35′40″S. 80°43′39″W. Driving snow at first. Brilliant afternoon. Gale dropping to breeze. Transverse sastrugi.

(6) 10 Nov. 94. Distance: 14.9 km. Total: 88.9 km. Altitude 900 m.

Overcast. Huge transverse sastrugi. Cross a ridge with wide crevasses. Generally on skis, but alternate a couple of hours between crampons and skis. Try radio, do not make contact. Camp 16.30 hours. Am exhausted.

(7) 11 Nov. 94. Distance: 18.8 km. Total: 107.7 km. Altitude 1130 m.

80°53′33″S. 80°28′31″W. Overcast and drift snow. Sastrugi. Hard.

(8) 12 Nov. 94. Distance: 22.9 km. Total: 130.6 km. Altitude 1130 m.

81°05′43″S. 80°19′23″W. Fine weather. Some patches without sastrugi. From gale to breeze.

(9) 13 Nov. 94. Distance: 23.5 km. Total: 154.1 km. Altitude 1120 m.

81°18′18″S. 80°18′10″W. Fine weather. Some patches without sastrugi. From gale to breeze.

(10) 14 Nov. 94. Distance: 25.3 km. Total: 179.4 km.

81°31′51″S. 80°22′09″W. Lightly clouded. A few sastrugi today. Fresh breeze, light gale.

(11) 15 Nov. 94. Distance: 27.8 km. Total: 207.2 km.

81°46′44″S. 80°20′54″W. Fine weather. Light breeze. Some stretches with huge sastrugi.

(12) 16 Nov. 94. Distance: 26.4 km. Total: 233.6 km. Altitude 1120 m.

82°00′52″S. 80°24′18″W. From whiteout to overcast. From light to stiff gale. Some stretches with sastrugi.

(13) 17 Nov. 94. Distance: 25.8 km. Total: 259.4 km. Altitude 900 m.

82°14′38″S. 80°14′54″W. From overcast to sunshine. From fresh breeze to gale. Huge transverse sastrugi.

(14) 18 Nov. 94. Distance: 25.9 km. Total: 285.3 km.

82°28′27″S. 80°15′30″W. Brilliant sunshine. Fresh breeze to gale. During the afternoon went up a ridge with crevasses, so I continued ten and a half hours before I found a camping site.

(15) 19 Nov. 94. Distance: 25.9 km. Total: 311.2 km. Altitude 1140 m.

82°56′50″S. 80°13′41″W. Brilliant sunshine. From breeze to stiff gale. Sastrugi.

(16) 20 Nov. 94. Distance: 27.1 km. Total: 338.3 km.

82°56′50″S. 80°13′41″W. From sunshine to clouded over. From breeze to gale. Sastrugi.

(17) 21 Nov. 94. Distance: 4.6 km. Total: 342.9 km.

82°59′15″S. 80°11′30″W. Ought to have remained in the tent. Gale at the start, which rose. Whirling snow gave zero visibility, but could see blue skies high above. Camped after two hours. Certainly took an hour to pitch tent. Drift snow everywhere. Storm and difficult to sleep.

(18) 22 Nov. 94. Distance: 25 km. Total: 367.9 km. Altitude 1200 m.

83°12′37″S. 80°17′29″W. Cloudy. From gale to breeze. Sastrugi.

(19) 23 Nov. 94. Distance: 27.8 km. Total: 395.7 km. Altitude 1230 m.

83°27′26″S. 80°36′08″W. Whiteout. Visibility the last few hours. Breeze. Few sastrugi.

(20) 24 Nov. 94. Distance: 29.8 km. Total: 425.5 km. Altitude 1200 m.

83°43′15″S. 80°34′56″W. Halcyon day for 5 hours. Light breeze, low sastrugi. Whiteout the last three hours.

(21) 25 Nov. 94. Distance: 29.1 km. Total: 454.6 km. Altitude 1190 m.

83°58′49″S. 80°32′54″W. Cloudy. Gale, sastrugi.

(22) 26 Nov. 94. Distance: 28.4 km. Total: 483.0 km. Altitude 1290 m.

84°14′02″S. 80°35′23″W. From cloudy to whiteout. Moderate breeze. The last two hours few sastrugi.

(23) 27 Nov. 94. Distance: 28.5 km. Total: 511.5 km. Altitude 1290 m.

84°29′18″S. 80°42′04″W. Five hours whiteout, five hours cloudy. Horribly sluggish because of snow/rime falling during whiteout.

(24) 28 Nov. 94. Distance: 21.2 km. Total: 532.7 km. Altitude 1290 m.

84°40′31″S. 80°28′44″W. Whole day alternating between whiteout and cloudy. When it cleared for an hour in the middle of the day I saw a ridge with crevasses a little way to the east. Camped 1700 hours. One of my skins fell off. Took it into the tent to dry it over the Primus and put on fresh glue.

(25) 29 Nov. 94. Distance: 27.5 km. Total: 560.2 km. Altitude 1350 m.

84°55′18″S. 80°29′44″W. Cloudy, which changed to sunshine. Saw Thiel Mountains! 2–5 cm. fresh snow. No sastrugi. Breeze. Mega sluggish.

(26) 30 Nov. 94. Distance: 26.2 km. Total: 586.4 km. Altitude 1170 m.

85°09′20″S. 80°34′35″W. Sunshine! Breeze. Sluggish because of fresh snow. Low sastrugi. I'm over halfway!

(27) 1 Dec. 94. Distance: 27.6 km. Total: 614.0 km. Altitude 1290 m.

85°24′06″S. 80°24′25″W. Clouded over, but halcyon afternoon with light breeze and brilliant sunshine. Sastrugi. Descend perceptibly into a little valley. The morrow can be hard. . . .

(28) 2 Dec. 94. Distance: 25.5 km. Total: 639.5 km. Altitude 1590 m.

85°37′40″S. 80°24′16″W. Sun. Fresh breeze to gale. Five hours up a ridge without sastrugi. Heavy going. Cold.

(29) 3 Dec. 94. Distance: 25.3 km. Total: 664.8 km. Altitude 1440 m.

85°50′53″S. 80°23′32″W. Sunshine. Fresh breeze to gale. Undulating landscape. Sastrugi. Cold.

(30) 4 Dec. 94. Distance: 24.8 km. Total: 689.6 km. Altitude 1710 m.

86°04′23″S. 80°20′37″W. Sunshine. Fresh breeze to gale. Undulating landscape. Sastrugi. Cold.

(31) 5 Dec. 94. Distance: 16.9 km. Total: 706.5 km. Altitude 1830 m.

86°13′28″S. 80°31′50″W. Heavy gale and driving snow all morning. Late start to wait for better weather. Wind and driving snow dropped somewhat and start around 11:30 a.m. Sastrugi and mega sluggish snow.

(32) 6 Dec. 94. Distance: 26.3 km. Total: 732.8 km. Altitude 2012 m.

86°27′28″S. 80°43′54″W. Sunshine. Mega sastrugi to begin with. The last four hours flat—without sastrugi! Undulating landscape.

(33) 7 Dec. 94. Distance: 24.3 km. Total: 757.1 km. Altitude 1950 m.

86°40′38″S. 80°43′19″W. Sunshine. Fresh breeze to gale. Undulating landscape. Two hours without skins!! Wonderful. Cold.

(34) 8 Dec. 94. Distance: 23.7 km. Total: 780.8 km. Altitude 1980 m.

86°53′10″S. 80°48′07″W. Sunshine. Wind rising to heavy gale. Climbed a ridge and broke through to thighs. Deep, blue crevasse. Cold.

(35) 9 Dec. 94. Distance: 24.4 km. Total: 805.2 km. Altitude 2160 m.

87°06′14″S. 80°40′32″W. Sunshine. Gale and mega sastrugi.

(36) 10 Dec. 94. Distance: 22.2 km. Total: 827.4 km. Altitude 2190 m.

87°18′10″S. 80°42′50″W. Sunshine. Fresh breeze. Mega sastrugi. Moved for several hours through labyrinths of sastrugi without skis.

(37) 11 Dec. 94. Distance: 24.3 km. Total: 851.7 km. Altitude 2610 m.

87°31′06″S. 80°42′44″W. Partly cloudy to clouded over. Fresh breeze-gale. Side of ridge with crevasses 2–5 meters wide. No sastrugi on uphill slopes. Otherwise mega sastrugi. Difficult to move on skis.

(38) 12 Dec. 94. Distance: 22.8 km. Total: 874.5 km. Altitude 2550 m.

87°43′28″S. 80°41′88″W. Partly clouded over. Fresh breeze, which rose. Four hours through mega sastrugi.

(39) 13 Dec. 94. Distance: 20.6 km. Total: 895.1 km. Altitude 2610 m.

87°54′21″S. 80°57′56″W. Sunshine. Moderate breeze,

rising. Heavy gale or more while I am writing diary. Five hours through mega sastrugi. Hard.

(40) 14 Dec. 94. Distance: 12.4 km. Total: 907.5 km. Altitude 2670 m.

88°00'58"S. 81°01'38"W. Clouded over and whiteout. Sastrugi. Cold. Two frostbitten fingers and camped around 1400 hours. Lit stove in tent to get warm. Good weather in the evening. Cessna from ANI circled once over me just before 10:00 p.m. Plane circled once again and managed to wave anorak.

(41) 15 Dec. 94. Distance: 23.5 km. Total: 931.0 km. Altitude 2610 m.

88°13'49"S. 80°55'10"W. Overcast. Fresh breeze. Smaller sastrugi. Sluggish drift snow.

(42) 16 Dec. 94. Distance: 22.2 km. Total: 953.2 km. Altitude 2580 m.

88°25'27"S. 81°16'09"W. Sunshine. Breeze. Cold. Last part of day flat.

(43) 17 Dec. 94. Distance: 19.5 km. Total: 972.7 km. Altitude 2730 m.

88°35'50"S. 81°32'25"W. Sunshine. Fresh breeze right in my face. Cold and sluggish.

(44) 18 Dec. 94. Distance: 22.7 km. Total: 995.4 km. Altitude 2730 m.

88°47'53"S. 80°04'35"W. Sunshine. Moderate breeze. Half the day without skins. Marvelous!

(45) 19 Dec. 94. Distance: 22.9 km. Total: 1018.3 km. Altitude 2700 m.

89°00′07″S. 79°22′59″W. Sunshine. Dead calm! Woke in the middle of the night and thought something was wrong, but it was dead calm! First entire day without skins. Flat—not a sastrugi! Snow crystals like ten-kroner coins. Cold. Drifted off course after having repaired compass mounting and set compass wrongly. Slovenly! Noticed it first at lunch, when sun was suddenly in an unaccustomed place.

(46) 20 Dec. 94. Distance: 23 km. Total: 1041.3 km. Altitude 2700 m.

89°12′21″S. 79°59′23″W. Sunshine. Dead calm and flat. Loose snow and sluggish.

(47) 21 Dec. 94. Distance: 24.3 km. Total: 1065.6 km. Altitude 2820 m.

89°25′24″S. 80°10′34″W. Sunshine. Dead calm and flat. Loose and sluggish.

(48) 22 Dec. 94. Distance: 24.6 km. Total: 1090.2 km. Altitude 2850 m.

89°38′19″S. 79°23′18″W. Sunshine. Breeze right in my face. Sastrugi and flat.

(49) 23 Dec. 94. Distance: 24.6 km. Total: 1114.8 km. Altitude 2850 m.

89°550′12″S. 83°16′00″W. Sunshine. Dead calm— breeze. Sastrugi and flat. Saw three black dots, South Pole as mirage.

(50) 24 Dec. 94. Distance: 18.3 km. Total: 1133.1 km. Altitude 2880 m.

89°59′42″S, 148°21′00″W is the position of my tent during my stay. Sunshine, dead calm. Caught sight of South Pole base 11:00 a.m., arrived 4:00 p.m. Feel in great form!

MENU

	Weight (g)	Calories per 100 grams	Calories per day	Total weight 50 days (kg)
Breakfast				
"Gull Frokost"	150	566	597	7.5
Dried cream (55 percent)	30	660	198	1.5
MCT/Soya bean oil	35	904	316	4.25
Rett i koppen (chocolate drink)	35	400	140	3.0
	(250)		(1,251)	
Lunch and brief stops				
"Gull Frokost Spesial"	100	383	383	5.0
Stratos (chocolate) with nuts	150	575	862	7.5
2 pieces Bixit chocolate	34	510	173	1.7
2 XL-1 (energy/ nutrition drink)	50	372	372	5.0
Marzipan	40	459	184	2.0
	(374)		(1,974)	

	Weight (g)	Calories per 100 grams	Calories per day	Total weight 50 days (kg)
Dinner				
Crushed potato chips	115	535	615	5.75
½ Blå Bånd vacuum-dried meal	79	480	379	4.0
Rett i koppen (chocolate drink)	25	400	120	1.25
Rett i koppen (black currant drink)	25	370	93	1.25
	(244)		(1,207)	
Total	**868 g**		**4,432 calories**	**49.7 kg**

Plus: vitamin pills, Mother's Kentucky cake, sweets

Minus: breakfast and between meals in hand on arrival at the South Pole

I assume my intake was between 3,800 and 4,400 calories per day.

I gained 10 kg (60,000 calories) before starting, and I lost 10 kg on the expedition.

EQUIPMENT LIST

Camping

Helsport two-man tent of ripstop nylon (3.6 kilos)
Sewn-in groundsheet covered with super-thin insulated mattress
2 Ridgeway mattresses
Ajungilak Denali sleeping bag fitted with zipper
Spade
Snow brush
Urine bottle
Personal tent bag
Toilet paper

Cooking

4 MSR 1-liter fuel tanks with pump
2 MSR XGK II burners, on Primus principle
1 Nansen cooker, 3-liter capacity, made by Norwegian Defense
    Research Institute
1 piece of thin plywood to steady burner
1 widemouthed food thermos
1 spoon
1 funnel for water
1 funnel for gasoline
1 steel thermos
2 plastic thermoses
Condiments

Matches
Storm matches
Zippo lighter

Walking/Skiing

Sled with cover fitted with Norwegian military closing system, the tubes of which served as spare ski poles
1 strong bungee strap
Alpine rope
6 carabiners (clip ring with spring-loaded gate originally used by mountaineers to hitch ropes to anchors for protection)
1 pair Åsnes skis with steel edges and wax-free base (Mohair strip insets)
Super Rottefella Telemark bindings with two Kandahar cables as backup
1 pair Swix ski poles
1 pair skins
Glue to attach skins
Lill-Sport combined bag and man-hauling harness with mounting for compass

Clothing

Microfiber windproof anorak with wolverine fur lining around hood
Microfiber windproof trousers
1 pair large Lill-Sport windproof outer mittens
1 pair woolen mittens
1 pair Harjo mittens
1 pair Medima gloves
1 pair Medima elbow warmers
1 pair Medima knee warmers
Medima back warmer

2 pairs Craft socks

2 pairs Harjo socks

2 pairs vapor barrier socks

1 pair Ajungilak bivouac boots

Lill-Sport "field cap"

Woolen cap

Neoprene earmuffs

Balaclava cap

Alfa ski boots—Mørdre model of Cordura uppers with Velcro surround

Lill-Sport snow gaiters

Felt insoles

Down jacket

Fleece jacket

Fleece trousers

2 Devold Aquadukt woolen vests

2 pairs Devold Aquadukt woolen long johns

Personal Equipment

Bollé sun goggles with nose protector

Bollé skiing goggles with yellow and red inserts

Face mask (Neoprene and plastic for skiing goggles)

Sector SGE watch

Barometer

3 hand warmers

Talcum powder

Diary

Peer Gynt by Henrik Ibsen

Anthology of poetry

Moist wipes

Toothbrush

Toothpaste

Dental floss

Toothpicks

Glacier Equipment

Instep crampons with four points

Carabiners and rope as indicated

1 snow anchor

2 ice screws with rope loop attached

Cameras and Film

Fuji film

Videotapes

Minox camera

Nikon camera

Sony Handycam 3CCD video camera

Spare batteries

Navigation, Safety, Communications

2 Trimble GPS Ensign satellite navigation sets

2 sets of 4 Energizer batteries

External battery lead

1 lithium battery pack, 12-V

2 "Sydpol" azimuth compasses

1 compass mounting

Map, 1:250,000 scale

General small-scale map

Argos

HF communications radio

First Aid

Needle and thread

Broad-spectrum antibiotics

Painkillers
Burn ointment
Dressing strips
Eye drops and ointment
Sunblock
Compeed tape for blisters
Adhesive bandages
Single component dental filling

Spares and Tools

Swiss Army knife
Leatherman multi-tool
Saddlemaker's needle for tent repairs
Safety pins
Parachute cords
Epoxy resin glue
Carbon sock hardened with contact cement, for ski repairs
Screws for ski bindings
Patent ski straps to improvise emergency bindings
Link joint to repair a broken tent hoop
Spoon
Contact glue
Ski pole basket

EXPLORERS TO THE
SOUTH POLE

Long before I could go to the South Pole myself, the old explorers first planted the thought in me to go, and through their stories they helped me on the way to the South Pole.

Fridtjof Nansen never realized his ambition of going to the South Pole, something he had begun to consider when he crossed Greenland in 1888. After his three-year Arctic drift in *Fram,* he was caught up in politics, first playing a leading role in the achievement of Norwegian independence from Sweden in 1905 and then turning to international humanitarian work, for which he was awarded the Nobel Peace Prize in 1922. Nansen was Roald Amundsen's model in planning and action. I have received a great deal of pleasure from his writings, but here I'll have to put him aside, as he never actually accomplished his dream of skiing to the South Pole. Those who did go to the Antarctic, and whose stories there made the deepest impression on me, were Douglas Mawson, Robert Falcon Scott, Ernest Shackleton, Otto Nordenskjöld, and, it almost goes without saying, Roald Amundsen.

Otto Nordenskjöld, 1901–3

Among the pioneering Antarctic expeditions at the turn of the century, one from Sweden was led by Otto Nordenskjöld. He was a nephew of the more famous Finnish-Swedish polar explorer

Adolf Erik Nordenskiöld, who sailed through the Northeast Passage in *Vega* in 1878–79 and also distinguished himself in Greenland and Svalbard.

In 1901, Otto Nordenskjöld sailed south in a whaler called *Antarctic*, commanded by the same Norwegian captain, C. A. Larsen, who had led the pioneering *Jason* expedition in 1892–93. That expedition didn't have much impact in Norway, but abroad it reawakened interest in Antarctica.

Nordenskjöld embarked on a scientific expedition to explore West Antarctica. Ice conditions prevented him from reaching Larsen's King Oscar II Land by ship as he had intended. After an exploratory cruise in the eastern Weddell Sea, Nordenskjöld, together with a small party, landed at Snow Hill Island and established winter quarters there. In October 1902, Nordenskjöld and two companions accomplished the first major Antarctic dogsled journey, across what is now called the Larsen Ice Shelf, a distance of 650 kilometers (400 miles). He expected to see the ship on his return, but it never arrived.

Antarctic had spent the winter in Patagonia, the Falklands, and South Georgia, where, incidentally, C. A. Larsen gave Grytviken its name. It means "Cauldron Inlet," which was derived from the cauldrons left by sealers, who had used them to render blubber. When the time came, difficult ice conditions prevented Larsen from fetching the landing party at Snow Hill Island. He sent three men off across the ice to tell Nordenskjöld that the ship was trapped in the ice and that he would have to prepare for another winter. The three men never reached their destination. Moving on skis and hauling a sled, they were stopped by open water and assumed therefore that *Antarctic* would reach the island after all. So, as previously agreed, they turned and went to Hope Bay, at the tip of the Antarctic Peninsula, to be picked up by the ship.

Weeks turned to months, and the men realized that something had gone wrong. They built a stone hut, using their sled as a roof. Inside, they pitched their tent for extra insulation. They lined the floor with penguin hides. For the most part, they lived off of penguins, killing 300 in all. Now and then they caught a fish or a seal. To keep their sanity during the winter, they established certain rules, which they kept rigorously. All three took turns cooking and thanked each other for doing so with the same formality they practiced at home. Furthermore, they took turns entertaining each other during the evenings. It is one of the unsung sagas of Antarctica.

Antarctic, meanwhile, remained stuck in the pack ice and began to leak. C. A. Larsen tried to beach the ship on Paulet Island but was driven the wrong way by the ice, wind, and currents. On February 12, 1903, *Antarctic* was crushed by the ice, and Larsen, together with nineteen men, just managed to get ashore on Paulet Island.

They too built a stone hut, but food was more important than shelter. Their only chance of survival was to slaughter as many penguins as possible before the birds migrated. Larsen and his companions endured harsh winter storms. They spent their evenings playing cards, singing, chatting, and reading aloud from the few books they had managed to salvage. Gallows humor concealed the fear of what was to become of them. Nobody knew where they were. Their dreams centered on food and rescue.

The Swedish expedition was now spread over three different places around the northern part of the Antarctic Peninsula. They were all cut off from outside help. Neither the ship's party nor the men marooned at Hope Bay were equipped for wintering.

In the southern spring of 1903, the three men from Hope Bay traveled across to Vega Island, where they had put a depot the previous year. They were aiming to reach Nordenskjöld at Snow Hill Island. By then the sea ice had broken up, and they were faced by open water, but they managed to continue on the fast ice along the coast of James Ross Island. They met seals along the way; one day they sighted some that appeared to be standing up, but they were actually human beings. One of them was Nordenskjöld—who, when he saw the filthy, bearded figures, thought he was confronted with another race of human beings. And they didn't recognize him, either. They began by speaking English; eventually the true state of affairs emerged. It was an emotional reunion.

Meanwhile, the shipwrecked party on Paulet Island somehow had to seek help. At the beginning of October, Larsen, together with three companions, rowed in an open boat to Hope Bay. It was a hard, stormy journey, made more dramatic by sleeping on ice floes that broke up beneath them. They reached Hope Bay on November 4 only to find it deserted, but the three castaways had left a message in a bottle, noting their intended route. Larsen and his men followed in their wake, rowing over Erebus and Terror Gulf.

When *Antarctic* failed to return to civilization as expected, relief expeditions were organized. The first to reach Snow Hill Island was from the Argentine, in a ship called *Uruguay*, under Captain Irizar. He arrived on November 8. Nordenskjöld's surprised delight was dampened by the fact that nothing had been seen or heard of *Antarctic*.

Late that same evening, the dogs suddenly began barking. Nordenskjöld couldn't find words to express his relief when he discovered that this racket was announcing the arrival of Larsen and his companions. The last part of their journey had been a long tramp of more than twenty kilometers over the sea ice. Nordenskjöld was even happier when he heard that the remainder of the crew was on Paulet Island. A few minutes earlier, he thought that the whole ship's company had perished. Having retrieved those at Snow Hill Island, *Uruguay* picked up the men on Paulet Island and returned safely to South America: a wonderful happy ending.

Robert Falcon Scott, 1901–4

Robert Falcon Scott was "headhunted" for the British National Antarctic Expedition in 1901–4 by Sir Clements Markham, the powerful and autocratic president of the Royal Geographical Society. The choice of Scott was a surprise to many people. He was a regular naval officer but according to one of his superiors had neither the knowledge nor the experience for polar exploration. From the start, promotion, fame, and glory drove Scott on his adventure in the south. Together with Sir Clements Markham, Scott visited Fridtjof Nansen at his home at Lysaker, on the outskirts of Oslo, to learn what he could about snow travel. Nansen gave sound advice on most things and emphasized in particular that planning was the most difficult part of any expedition.

In January 1902, Scott berthed his expedition ship, *Discovery*, in winter quarters off a promontory that was later named Hut Point, on Ross Island, in McMurdo Sound, at the southwestern extremity of the Ross Sea. Among those on this expedition were Dr. Edward Wilson, nicknamed Bill, who subsequently also joined Scott's second expedition of 1910–13, and Ernest Shackleton, who also was to distinguish himself in the Antarctic. At the end of August 1902, the expedition started to practice dog driving. No one had any experience with dogs as draft animals, nor could they learn to drive them properly.

On November 2, Scott, Shackleton, and Wilson set off for the South Pole. Had they been more experienced, better prepared, and luckier, with better food for the dogs, they might conceivably have reached the South Pole. The dogs determined the speed of travel and time on the march. Usually one day's travel didn't exceed six or seven kilometers. Scott blamed the dogs' poor performance on their fodder: dried fish (from Norway) that had supposedly spoiled on the voyage south. Out of kindness to animals, he killed as few seals as possible for dog food!

He also mistakenly believed that the dogs' poor performance was due to their inability to face strong winds and drifting snow.

They were forced to turn back on New Year's Day 1903, 830 kilometers (520 miles) from the Pole, 372 kilometers (230 miles) farther south than anyone had previously gone. The return journey took place without dogs, and Shackleton fell ill along the way. He had a fever and coughed up blood but refused to allow himself to be hauled on the sled. After ninety-three days and 1,090 kilometers (680 miles), they returned to *Discovery* on February 3.

During and after this journey, there was friction between Scott and Shackleton; in Wilson, Scott found a constant friend and companion in the field. The expedition had a muted reception in England, but Scott did obtain his much-coveted promotion to captain, besides various medals and decorations.

Ernest Shackleton, 1907–9

Ernest Shackleton came home quite ill from the *Discovery*, but he had one thought in his head: the South Pole. Scott had the same idea, but Shackleton set off first. His main sponsor was his employer, Scottish industrialist William Beardmore. There were rumors that Beardmore's wife was rather too interested in Shackleton, and by sending him off to the Antarctic, Beardmore got rid of his rival.

After the miserable southern journey of 1902–3, Shackleton no longer trusted dogs. He did take nine dogs but put his faith in Siberian ponies, which had previously been used on an English expedition to Franz Josef Land. He also took the first powered vehicle to Antarctica, a specially built, fifteen-horsepower Arrol-Johnston motorcar, adapted to snow travel. It could move only on a hard surface and was limited to short distances.

Establishing his base near Scott's old winter quarters at Hut Point, in McMurdo Sound, Shackleton began his polar journey on

November 3, 1908, together with Jameson Boyd Adams, Dr. Eric Marshall, and Frank Wild. Almost from the beginning, hunger was their constant companion, coupled with the fear of falling to their death in a crevasse. On several occasions, they did fall into crevasses, along with their ponies, but miraculously hauled each other out again.

Each man had a sled drawn by a pony. After three weeks, the animals began to fail, and in the fifth week the last pony, Socks, vanished in a chasm on the Beardmore Glacier. Shackleton and his companions now had to man-haul up the glacier, each sled weighing 120 kilos (264 pounds). They reached the polar plateau on Christmas Eve. They met bad weather and deep cold and were weatherbound, meagerly rationing their food, for three weeks. On January 9, 1909, they reached 88°23′ and turned back 175 kilometers (109 miles) from the South Pole. The return journey became a race against death. Their depots contained too little food, and, more dead than alive, they were picked up by the expedition ship *Nimrod* in McMurdo Sound after having traveled for 128 days with food for only ninety-three days.

Shackleton had shown the way to the South Pole. He could have attained his goal, at the cost of risking the lives of the whole party on the way back, thus becoming the hero that Scott was to be. He chose instead to turn around before it was too late. His journey gave Amundsen and Scott vital information.

This expedition also produced another great exploit in the first attainment of the South Magnetic Pole. Three men hauled heavy sleds over a thousand kilometers (625 miles) to the invisible point then in South Victoria Land and back again. One of them was the Australian Douglas Mawson.

In contrast to Scott, Shackleton was a charismatic leader whose followers both respected and loved him. He had the common touch and lost not a single man on any of the expeditions he led. Like Scott, dreams of fame and fortune drew him to the

Antarctic and glorious failures rather than successes made his reputation.

Of Scott's and Shackleton's first expeditions, Amundsen said, "The English must have had bad dogs, or they did not understand how to use them. . . . The English had loudly proclaimed for all the world that skis and dogs are useless in these regions, and that fur clothes are nonsense. We will see, we will see."

Roald Amundsen, 1910–11

Roald Amundsen became the first person to reach the South Pole on December 14, 1911, together with four companions. His story tells of drama before the expedition—a kind of drama that I, who went solo, was luckily spared. At Amundsen's base, Framheim, the drama that unfolded was to have tragic consequences. Nine men spent the southern winter of 1911 there completing their preparations. After a start too early in the spring and a forced retreat, the idyll was broken. Amundsen had proved to be a leader who could not admit his mistakes.

Hjalmar Johansen, four years older than the thirty-eight-year-old Amundsen, was the most experienced polar traveler at Framheim. He had been to university and was once a full-time army officer, besides being an all-around sportsman. During the *Fram* expedition of 1893–96, he was Nansen's chosen companion on the ski and sled journey toward the North Pole. They reached latitude 86°14′ north and on their return southward spent their celebrated winter in the hut on Franz Josef Land. As a result, Nansen and Johansen became living legends. Even though they enjoyed a liberal dose of luck, their journey was an extraordinary achievement.

Johansen had been bitten by the polar bug and subsequently joined several expeditions to Svalbard. After the expedition with Nansen, however, he became an alcoholic. He left the army, his marriage broke up, and he went bankrupt. Hoping that another expedition would restore Johansen to an even keel, Nansen compelled Amundsen, against his own better judgment, to take Johansen along on the journey.

Since childhood, Amundsen had dreamed of being a polar explorer, and he ended his medical studies to realize his dream. He went sealing in the Arctic to gain experience and took his mate's certificate. He joined the Belgica expedition of 1897–99, the first to winter in the Antarctic. The leader was a Belgian, Adrien de Gerlache, and Dr. Frederick A. Cook, who later claimed to have reached the North Pole, was also on the expedition. A cosmopolitan crew survived a harsh and trying winter, suffering great hardship.

In 1906, when Amundsen returned home after having become the first man to sail through the Northwest Passage in his tiny sloop *Gjøa,* he became an instant hero among his countrymen in the newly independent Norway and in the rest of the world as well. To plant the flag in the most inaccessible parts of the globe was the great sporting deed of the age, and those who carried it out achieved a status that can be compared only with that of our own sporting heroes.

On the South Pole expedition, Amundsen and Johansen were the two most experienced men. For a long time, they had been getting on each other's nerves: Amundsen was an authoritarian leader, and Johansen had a quick temper and low self-esteem but nonetheless considered himself the more experienced of the two. At Framheim, Amundsen increasingly felt his authority threatened by Johansen, and finally, this conflict erupted, with devastating consequences for Johansen.

Amundsen was straining at the leash. He had challenged Scott to a race and wanted to start for the Pole as soon as possible. He set his departure for September 8, 1911, early in the southern spring. Johansen had repeatedly warned Amundsen against starting too early, because it would be too cold for both men and dogs. But Amundsen could think only of winning the race. What happened during those September days is recorded in Johansen's diaries (found in an Oslo hotel in 1932), but nothing about his conflict with Amundsen was published until 1961, in a Norwegian biography of Johansen.

Amundsen and his men had to turn back on September 12, after only four days. The temperature had dropped to −55 degrees Celsius (−67 degrees Fahrenheit). The dogs suffered from the cold, and several died on the return journey. Two men, Helmer Hansen and Kristian Prestrud, had frostbitten heels. It was so cold that the liquid in the compasses froze solid. Amundsen went back with the first returning sled; the rest of his men had to manage as best they could. "I was even more astonished at this singular way of traveling in such terrain and at a temperature of 51 degrees," Johansen wrote in his diary. Johansen probably saved Prestrud's life by forcing him to travel all night until they reached Framheim. To leave men to their own devices without food, drink, or fuel in more than −50 degrees Celsius (−58 degrees Fahrenheit) could have ended in disaster. Amundsen returned to Framheim at four o'clock in the afternoon; the last dog team arrived after midnight.

At breakfast the next morning came the confrontation he had long feared. Within everyone's hearing, Johansen criticized Amundsen for having abandoned two men out on the ice shelf without food or fuel. He accused Amundsen of poor leadership and panic. The majority agreed with Johansen but dared not say so out loud.

In the course of that day, Amundsen changed the composition of the polar party: to Johansen's almost unbearable disappointment, he was removed from the polar party, and he and Prestrud were told instead to explore King Edward VII Land. Johansen tried to apologize for his outburst, but Amundsen felt that he had to establish his leadership once and for all. Amundsen wrote in his diary that the bull had to be taken by the horns by making an example out of Johansen and that the journey to the South Pole could not include any critical persons. With hindsight, Amundsen justified the early start on the grounds that he had put men and equipment to the test, besides transporting extra supplies to the depot at 80° south. But all the surviving diaries record a miserable and gruesome atmosphere at Framheim after the false start.

In spite of everything, some good emerged. The men did put themselves to the test. Their boots still proved unsatisfactory and, for the fourth and last time, were modified. Most important, the polar party was reduced to five, while the depots had been calculated for eight men, which gave a good margin of safety.

At long last, on October 19, 1911, the polar party finally set off on what was to become the most famous sled journey in the world. The members were Helmer Hansen, Oscar Wisting, Sverre Hassel, Olav Bjaaland, and Roald Amundsen, and they took four sleds, each drawn by thirteen dogs. The climb up to the polar icecap via the Axel Heiberg Glacier took only four days against an allotted ten. The dogs were driven hard. It was a grim moment when twenty-four animals had to be shot on the icecap, according to plan, because no more food had been taken for them and they were to serve as fodder for their companions on the way back. The place was called the Butcher's Shop. The whole route was marked with two-meter-high snow cairns in order to secure a safe, quick return. In all, 150 cairns were built, each numbered and labeled with the course back to the next one.

On December 14, at three o'clock in the afternoon, the distance meters on all three sleds indicated that they had reached the South Pole. All five men held the flag when it was planted in the snow. After precise observations, however, the Pole was found to be a little way off, and on December 16 the men encircled it.

A tent was pitched there, with a little Norwegian flag flying from the top. Inside the tent, Amundsen left a small bag with a letter to Scott and another to King Haakon, the Norwegian sovereign. The tent was dubbed "Polheim."

The homeward journey began on December 17, and on January 25 Amundsen and his companions, with two sleds and eleven dogs, returned to Framheim. In all, they had covered 2,640 kilometers (1,650 miles) in ninety-nine days. Oscar Wisting summed up the journey thus: "Our task has been carried out; the best planned and executed polar expedition that has ever set out." Amundsen, after being criticized for having beaten Scott to the Pole, commented, "Victory awaits those who have everything in order—it is called good luck. Defeat is absolutely certain for those who have neglected to take the necessary precautions in time—this is called bad luck."

On the way home after the expedition, Johansen asked to be discharged at Hobart, Tasmania, and sailed on an English ship. For his part, Amundsen wrote home that he had been compelled to discharge Johansen at Hobart because he had been guilty of mutiny. Johansen kept silent over his treatment by Amundsen. In a newspaper interview after his homecoming, Johansen said of Amundsen, "With a leader like him, everything had to go well." But after his return from the Antarctic, Johansen was a broken man. On January 2, 1913, he took his own life.

Robert Falcon Scott, 1910–11

While Shackleton was nearly reaching the South Pole in 1909, Robert Falcon Scott had been at home in England, defending himself against criticism of the poor scientific results of his expedition of 1902–4. In addition, he was involved with Kathleen Bruce, a sculptress, whom he then married. In September 1909, after his son Peter was born, Scott began serious preparations for another Antarctic expedition. He and Kathleen went to Norway to test a newly designed motor sled. There, Scott met Nansen and was introduced to another Norwegian named Tryggve Gran, whom he recruited as a skiing expert for the expedition.

While in Norway, Scott tried in vain to meet Amundsen. He had hoped that he and Amundsen, in the Antarctic and Arctic respectively, could undertake simultaneous magnetic observations and, to that end, was prepared to offer instruments. In October 1910, when Scott was in Melbourne, on his way to Antarctica, he learned that Amundsen had changed plans and, instead of going north, was heading south instead. That marked the start of the race.

On the voyage from New Zealand to Antarctica, Scott's ship, *Terra Nova*, just survived a hurricane, thanks to heroic efforts on the part of the second in command, Lieutenant "Teddy" Evans. Scott named his winter quarters Cape Evans in his honor. This was in Scott's old haunts on Ross Island, in McMurdo Sound. Scott and his men, including Tryggve Gran, immediately started laying depots with dogs and ponies. Things went badly. Once again, ponies proved ill-adapted to the conditions, and they were in poor shape after the difficult ocean crossing.

Meanwhile, *Terra Nova*, which was making for King Edward VII Land, met *Fram* at the Bay of Whales. The Englishmen were invited aboard and also visited Amundsen's base at Framheim. The two expeditions conducted a kind of psychological warfare against each other. Amundsen wanted to hear about Scott's motor sleds, about which his interlocutors boasted, hinting that they were probably by then well on their way over the ice shelf. For their part, the Englishmen were impressed by the Norwegians' dog-driving abilities.

Terra Nova broke off her voyage eastward to return to Cape Evans and report that *Fram* was at the Bay of Whales. Scott and his men didn't take the news as calmly as the official reports suggest. One of the men, Apsley Cherry-Garrard, recorded that in an outburst of fury, Scott wanted to go over and fight Amundsen!

The English considered the Antarctic, and the South Pole in particular, to be their preserve. In their opinion, Scott led the way, but they completely ignored the fact that it was a Norwegian, Carsten Borchgrevink, one of the first to set foot on the Antarctic continent and the first to winter there, who was the real pioneer. Borchgrevink led an Antarctic expedition, mostly with Norwegians but under the British flag, between 1898 and 1900. His accomplishments were belittled and ignored both in Norway and by the Royal Geographical Society in England. When Scott was in Norway, incidentally, Borchgrevink advised him to start from the Bay of Whales. In that way, Scott would have been a hundred kilometers (sixty-two miles) closer to the South Pole.

On October 24, 1911, Teddy Evans set off in command of the advance party on the polar journey, a week before Scott himself. The use of two motor sleds caused delays, and both were abandoned after a week. Scott had followed Shackleton's example and put his faith in Siberian ponies. They hauled 250 kilos (550 pounds) each but couldn't withstand the conditions as well as expected, and eventually all were put down.

Scott didn't select the final polar party before January 3, 1912. By then they had reached 87°43′ south. Not everyone was equally keen to go on. To accompany him, Scott chose a naval petty officer named Edgar Evans, Dr. Edward Wilson ("Uncle Bill"), "Birdie" Bowers, and Captain L. E. G. Oates. Those who returned were Teddy Evans and two other petty officers, Lashly and Crean. Teddy Evans fell victim to scurvy and snow blindness and survived by the skin of his teeth. (Evans was later ennobled, took the title of Lord Mountevans, was a hero in both world wars, married a Norwegian, and died in his mountain cabin in Norway in 1957.)

The polar party was in reasonably good spirits on January 16, 1912, about thirty kilometers (nineteen miles) from their goal.

They were all on skis, except for Bowers, struggling along in the loose snow. He first sighted a cairn with a flag left by Amundsen. The shock was great, but some of the party, Oates in particular, showed great resilience. At this point Scott wrote in his diary the much-quoted words, "Great God! This is an awful place."

Scott must have recognized at an early stage in the journey that he would have trouble carrying out his intentions. All planning seems to have been based on the best possible conditions. He repeatedly declared that "under favourable circumstances" he would have avoided many of his difficulties.

One of the support parties, using dog teams, was ordered to continue sixteen days longer than planned. It also seems peculiar that an advance party went on nearly to the end. The upshot was that both groups used up precious supplies intended for the final party, and for both, the homeward march became a race against death. Scott had increased his polar party to five men, while everything had been organized for four. In retrospect, it's incredible that Scott was puzzled over the lack of food and fuel on the return journey.

Scott maintained until the end, and it is generally accepted, that he nearly got through alive. He was only sixteen kilometers (ten miles) from his main supplies at One Ton Depot, but in what state? Two of his companions were already dead. Edgar Evans had collapsed mentally, and Oates hobbled along the last few days before he left the tent to die. His legs were black with frostbite and hardly supported him any longer. Those who remained in the tent had serious frostbite. It is scarcely credible that these dying men were dragging sixteen kilos (thirty-five pounds) of fossils. It was not only with hindsight that Scott was wrong. He had ignored the fundamental rules of all the successful polar explorers of his own times: dogs, fur clothes, skis, and fresh meat.

Ernest Shackleton, 1914–17

Meanwhile, Shackleton was at home, waiting for the outcome of the race for the South Pole. When he heard that Amundsen had won, he conceived a plan by which the British might triumph over the Norwegians. The last remaining great polar exploit was the crossing of Antarctica, and that is what Shackleton proposed to carry out. His idea was to start from the Weddell Sea and finish at the Ross Sea, passing the South Pole on the way.

The main party was to sail into the Weddell Sea, while a support group was to go to the Ross Sea and put out depots to the Beardmore Glacier, where the two were to meet. Shackleton had relatively little trouble raising funds—or credit—and 5,000 hopefuls applied to join the expedition. In his ship *Endurance*, Shackleton sailed from England just as World War I was breaking out in August 1914. He offered his ship and crew to the navy but was told by then First Lord of the Admiralty Winston Churchill to continue the expedition as planned.

At Grytviken, in South Georgia, Shackleton was warned against continuing south because of particularly difficult ice conditions that season. By the beginning of December, he could wait no longer and sailed nonetheless. He had much to contend with and after a month hadn't even crossed the Polar Circle. In January 1915, the ship became trapped in the ice after a storm, only 350 meters (380 yards) from open water. For seven months, *Endurance* was beset until, in November, she was finally crushed by the ice pack despite desperate attempts to save her.

Shackleton now had only one ambition: to get everyone home alive. He had all his supplies and dogs and three lifeboats. After a frustrated attempt to reach land, Shackleton and his men settled down on a floe and drifted northward with the pack ice. Eventually, in April 1916, they reached the edge of the pack ice, the floes broke up, and they took to the boats. Then followed a fight for survival in perilous drift ice. Occasionally, they were able to rest on a floe. Drinking water ran out. Gales and driving snow swept over them. With heavy seas and temperatures well below zero, they were soaked and frozen stiff. Many became apathetic; some wanted to jump into the sea.

On April 15, after a whole week of struggle, they reached Elephant Island. This consisted of rock and ice, but there was plenty of drinking water and, with penguins and seals along the shore, food as well. They had not had solid ground underfoot for 445 days. With the help of two of the boats, they contrived a hut, depending on blubber stoves for heating, cooking, and lighting.

Shackleton decided to sail to South Georgia to seek help. Together with five companions, he set off in one of the lifeboats, named *James Caird* after a supporter of the expedition. The *James Caird* was exactly twenty-two feet long; somehow she survived seventeen days in the stormiest seas in the world before finally reaching South Georgia on May 10, 1916. This feat has gone down in history as Shackleton's open boat journey, one of the great sagas of the sea.

Unfortunately, Shackleton had landed at King Haakon Bay, on the uninhabited south shore of the island. The whaling stations he had been heading for lay on the other side, separated by mountains and glaciers. His boat was too weakened to attempt sailing around, so he decided to cross overland. On May 18 he set off with two companions, carrying food, rope, and ice axes but no sleeping bags. On May 20, they reached the Stromness whaling station, nearly at the end of their tether, having slept only once for a few minutes in the open. Shackleton had not slept at all.

At Stromness, the whalers were astounded to see Shackleton, certain that he had long since perished. The Norwegian whaler *Samson* sailed round to fetch the three men who had stayed behind at King Haakon Bay. On August 30, after various setbacks, Shackleton finally returned to Elephant Island in a small Chilean steamer called *Yelcho,* four months after sailing off on the open boat journey. He found everyone alive and well and rescued all of them.

The Ross Sea party, meanwhile, were also in difficulty. In their ship, *Aurora,* they sailed to Cape Evans, on Ross Island, and one group immediately began putting out depots on the ice shelf. On their return, in March 1915, the ice in McMurdo Sound had gone out, and they had to take shelter in Scott's old hut at Hut Point. Eventually, when the sea had frozen over again, they made their way back to Cape Evans, only to find that *Aurora* had been blown out to sea with most of the equipment and many of her crew. Luckily, Scott's expedition had left supplies, which the marooned men used for survival. Somehow, in the southern summer of 1915–16, they managed to put out the remainder of Shackleton's depots, up to the foot of the Beardmore Glacier. Blizzards sapped their strength on the return journey. One man died, and two more disappeared trying to reach Cape Evans from Hut Point before the sea ice was safely frozen. At last, on January 10, 1917, Shackleton arrived in *Aurora* to bring the survivors home. He was greatly saddened by the three deaths.

Forty years passed before Sir Vivian Fuchs made the first trans-Antarctic crossing with his motor vehicles. But the first one to cross with men and dogs, as Shackleton would have traveled, had to wait until 1990–91, when the Norwegian expedition under the two Mødre brothers crossed the continent with the motto "Shackleton's Dream."

When World War I was over, Shackleton wanted to return to the polar region. In 1921, he sailed once more for the Antarctic in a sealer, bought in Norway and renamed *Quest.* The purpose of this expedition was vague. On January 4, 1922, while the ship lay at Grytviken, Shackleton went to bed early to rest after the crossing of the Southern Ocean. He had been feeling ill for some time, and that last evening, while one of the expedition doctors was in his cabin, Shackleton suddenly had a massive heart attack. He died soon after and was buried in Grytviken; like many other explorers, the wild outlands had been his only true home on earth.

Liv Arnesen is a world-renowned explorer, lecturer, author, and educator. She and Ann Bancroft founded Bancroft Arnesen Explore, a nonprofit dedicated to global water sustainability, with expeditions planned through 2027 to raise awareness through education and storytelling. She and Bancroft are coauthors of *No Horizon Is So Far: Two Women and Their Historic Journey across Antarctica* (Minnesota, 2019). She lives near Oslo, Norway.

Ann Bancroft is one of the world's preeminent polar explorers and the first woman to reach both the North and South Poles. An internationally recognized educator, speaker, and philanthropist, she founded the Ann Bancroft Foundation in 1991. She lives near St. Paul, Minnesota.

Roland Huntford has written many books about polar exploration, including critically acclaimed biographies of Ernest Shackleton and Fridtjof Nansen as well as *The Last Place on Earth: Scott and Amundsen's Race to the South Pole.*